Best Wishes
to
Don

from Barbara Lumb

THE SPEN VALLEY STORY

CONTENTS:

i

FOREWORD:

In 2007, I came to live in the Spen Valley. On my first walk with Nina the labrador, I came across a little graveyard with four 17th Century graves in a copse of trees. I started to find out what the story was behind this little graveyard and in doing so became immersed in the history of the area. I discovered stories about Robin Hood and his death at the hands of his kinswoman, the Prioress of Kirklees Priory; about Charlotte Bronte who used the dramatic story of the Luddite attack on a local mill in one of her novels and who loved the Spen Valley and the friends she made here. And about the many characters who turned the Valley into a thriving industrial area.

As a retired history teacher, I felt the need to share my research and so this book aims to tell the story of the people of the Spen Valley from the very earliest times to the present day. I hope that this will help those living here have a greater understanding of how the landscape has developed the way it has and how events in our history have produced an independent-minded breed of folk who have had an impact not only on West Yorkshire but on a much wider area. There have been many books written about the towns and cities which surround the Spen Valley: Leeds, Bradford, Halifax and Wakefield, but very few which have told the story about the 'bit in the middle.' It is my opinion that this area has a rich heritage and an identity which demands a study all of its own.

THE HISTORY OF THE SPEN VALLEY

The Spen is a tiddler of a river as rivers go. It is only nine miles in length from its source just outside Bradford to the point where it enters the much larger River Calder. This history is about the hamlets and villages and towns which sit on the hillsides of this valley. It also includes, because of the way the medieval manors developed, a number of settlements on neighbouring valleys and hillsides and so the area being described is really much of the land that lies between the large towns and cities of West Yorkshire.

CHAPTER 1: THE BEGINNINGS

THE FIRST PEOPLE

Prehistoric Man made his home on the hillsides above the Calder Valley. The circular basin that was formed by the River Calder was the site of a glacial lake which geologists call Lake Calderdale. The waters of its tributaries, like the River Spen, flowed into this lake. River valleys like the River Calder and the River Spen would have been used as trade routes.

Very little is known about the earliest people who lived here but we do know that they were hunters using tools and weapons made from stone, antlers and bone and that the land they inhabited was thickly forested and the valleys were very boggy.

The technique of smelting iron came to Britain around 700 BC. This completely new technology was brought from Southern Europe by a people called the Celts who had begun migrating here. The Iron Age changed everything because here in the Spen Valley, as elsewhere, iron could be forged into axes and ploughs. Forests could be cleared. The heavy clay soils of the valleys could be cultivated and farmsteads and small self-sufficient villages began to appear. These were often near to rivers but they were mainly built on higher ground.

Common to this time were Iron Age hill forts. The nearest to us is the one at Castle Hill. This 900 feet high hill was the site of a major hill fort around 555 BC. Its main function though was not defence but as a settlement and a meeting place. It is very likely that there were hilltop settlements in the Spen Valley too, for example on Hartshead Moor.

By about 100 BC there were lots of different Celtic tribes living throughout Britain all led by warrior kings, but in 54 BC a Roman Army arrived to take over Celtic Britain with Julius Caesar at its head. This army was not here for long and Caesar himself returned to Rome after only three months, but several towns had been built in the South of England.

In the north and west the invasion had very little impact. By the 1st Century AD the hill forts had again become the gathering points for the worship of Pagan gods and for feasting and exchanging goods.

THE ROMAN INVASION

By AD 43 the Roman troops were back again, led by the Emperor Claudius and this time they were an un-stoppable force. Their aim was to conquer the whole of Britain.

The Celtic tribes put up fierce resistance as the invaders moved northwards. The hill forts now became places of defence but the Roman Army had a new weapon, the deadly crossbow and gradually they overcame all resistance and Britain became part of the Roman Empire. The Roman conquest was not easily achieved. It was more of a slow steady move northwards. Everywhere they conquered, the Romans had to build an infrastructure of roads and garrisons. Once the military structure was in place, they built towns, so it actually took them two decades to reach the north. The City of York, built in AD 71, is our nearest Roman city.

The only legacy of the Roman infrastructure in the Spen Valley is their road system. It is quite an amazing fact that we still have the route of a Magna Via passing through our 21st Century valley. In fact this road is part of the highway that took Roman troops from York to Chester. This important road ran through Wakefield and Dewsbury to Heckmondwike where it crossed the River Spen at a ford. It then continued through Hightown to Hartshead Moor and then down to the River Calder at Brighouse where it crossed the river.

One of the intriguing pieces of evidence for this being a Roman road is a field name on a 1612 Tithe map which is marked Street Pasture, the name always indicating a field abutting a Roman road. This former field is on the present day street called Aquila Way at Hightown. Another name for Hare Park Lane was Aquila Lane. This name could also be an indicator of Roman presence.

Aquila is the Latin name for eagle. The eagle was the symbol of a Roman Legion and as such was the most famous of the Roman Standards or banners. It was carried at the head of a legion formation when on the march and was fiercely protected on and off the field of battle. The Aquila emblem had up-raised wings surrounded by a laurel wreath. But there is no proof that this name signifies anything as it could simply be a family name. Roman roads would have been regarded by the Celts as being quite an awesome sight. Roads such as this one following the top of the escarpment, were an important means of controlling the area by making it easier to move troops quickly from place to place. This remained the most significant highway for hundreds of years. We now know it as the A649 Halifax Road.

Apart from their road system, we know too that the Romans smelted iron ore at Low Moor and that they built a fort near what was to be a Priory at Kirklees. A few Roman artefacts have been discovered, for example an Ampora dug up near the site of Liversedge Hall.

By about 200 AD, and after the military campaigns, most of the population remained rural but Britain had been changed by the Romans. There were written records and names and dates for the first time. The Celtic gods gave way to Roman gods and finally, after AD 313, to Christianity and the belief in one God.

But by AD 410, the Roman Empire was collapsing. The Spen Valley, like other parts of Britain, returned to the ways of the past.

During the 3rd Century AD, Saxon pirates had begun to raid the east coast of Britain and may even have settled along the coast during the Roman Occupation, but after the Roman legions were withdrawn during the early part of the 5th Century AD, groups of Anglo-Saxon invaders began to penetrate inland from the east coast and by around 700 AD had occupied nearly the whole of England. Vikings too raided the coast throughout the 8th Century and by the late 9th Century all these new immigrants had reached the Spen Valley, travelling up the rivers from the Humber Estuary.

Spen Valley Topography and Settlements

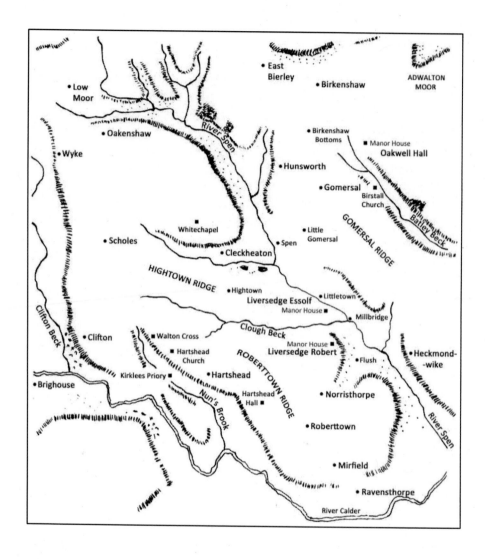

CHAPTER 2: THE EARLY MIDDLE AGES: 500 - 1066 AD

THE ANGLO-SAXON AND VIKING INVASIONS

Anglo-Saxon is the term used to describe the invading Germanic tribes who, over time, created the English Nation. The Angles may have come fron Angelm, a place in modern Germany. They gave their name to England. The Saxons came from Lower Saxony in modern Germany.

This movement of peoples was all part of a general migration from what is now North Germany and Southern Scandinavia. Their language, therefore comes from German dialects and this became the basis of the English language.

The Vikings added their language and culture as they reached these parts of Yorkshire. The Vikings came from Norway and Denmark. The Norwegian Vikings travelled round the coast of Scotland settling in parts of Scotland, Ireland and the west coast of England. It was the Danish Vikings who arrived on the east coast of England and who travelled up the rivers of Yorkshire and settled in parts of the Spen Valley.

We do have some interesting reminders of these invaders:

The Walton Cross

The Anglo-Saxons called the Celts foreigners or Weales and the place they lived in was a Ton. This gives us the name of one of the most fascinating relics of this period, the Walton Cross. This literally means the Cross at the Farmstead of the Foreigners; the Weale-ton or Walton. There is still a house on the site of that ancient farm.

The Walton Cross was originally a 15 foot high cross; probably coloured, built on the escarpment, a little way from where Hartshead Church now stands. It overlooks both the Calder and the Colne Valleys and would have been visible for miles around.

It may have been a Saxon preaching cross for the purpose of open-air religious services prior to a church being built, or even a boundary stone (the cross is on the ancient boundary of Liversedge on what was once Church Common Road and is now called Windy Bank Lane). In fact early documents refer to it as the Wagenstan or Way-Stone.

Only the base of the cross remains. It is made of millstone grit and stands about 1.5m high. There is ornamentation on each side.

The west face of the base has a central panel with a circle of knots and interlaced trefoils. The east face is the most richly decorated and includes a centre panel enclosed by a border of plaiting and roll and barley twist moulding.

Within the panel is a Tree of Life with spiral branches emerging horizontally from a central stem. There are faint traces of two bird forms on either side of the tree.

Walton Cross, Hartshead on its high escarpment.

This style of decoration shows the Scandinavian influence as the Tree of Life reflected Norse mythology; the tree being the one which sheltered the Norse gods in heaven. The style dates it to the late 9th or early 10th Centuries.

What is not clear is the actual function of the cross. But it does point to the fact that this part of Hartshead Moor was precisely that type of hilly terrain loved by early communities as a meeting place for choosing their chieftains, paying their taxes, solving disputes and holding fairs, as well as a place for open-air worship.

There were fewer than fifty high crosses erected in the country and so this one is very important. Particularly because it is on the same site where it has always been. These crosses provide an insight into the art of the time and the way the Anglo-Saxons used Scandinavian art forms.

It also provides us with evidence about their religious beliefs and meeting places. It is certainly a very important artefact from Anglo-Saxon times and is now a Grade II* listed monument, scheduled by English Heritage as a monument of national importance.

The Saxon Stone at Birstall Church

Another stone base can be found inside St Peter's Church in Birstall where it has been placed for safekeeping. This possibly dates from the late 10th Century. It also depicts the Tree of Life pattern but it is much simpler in design than the Walton Cross.

Place Name Evidence

Most of the present Spen Valley names owe their existence to this period.

Gomersal was Guthmer's Halh (hall) which means a dwelling in a sheltered place. Hunsworth was Hund's Enclosure. Names ending with Royd or Ley show where there were clearings made in dense woods.

A little group of huts would be a Ton as in Cleckheaton: the town on the heath. A Wick was a camp; so Heckmondwike was a place of refuge in the forest, fortified with an earthwork enclosure.

The origin of the name Liversedge is more difficult to understand.

It is possible that it comes from Sedge; the swampy ground in the valley and Leofhere's Ridge meaning the higher slopes.

Place names ending in Shaw indicate woodland clearings. Oakenshaw and Birkenshaw not only tell us that woodland has been cleared for a small settlement, but what type of woodland; oak and birch.

In fact what we now refer to as Birkenshaw Bottoms was the original village of Birkenshaw or the Birch Grove because this was on a sheltered south facing lower slope of a much higher ridge of land.

Anglian settlers came here from about the 6th Century.

The whole area was mainly settled by Saxons and Angles but at the confluence of the Spen and the Calder, there was a Danish settlement at Ravens Wharf and Ravensthorpe, the raven being part of the Danish flag. This indicates the landing place of the Vikings who displayed the raven as a bird of evil omen.

Other Scandinavians settled at North Bierley (Steinulfr), Wyke (Vestarr) and Hartshead (Anbjorn). The name Scholes comes from the Scandinavian word Skali meaning hut or shieling.

These place names show how early settlers made Royds or clearings and gradually began cultivating the fringes of the valley sides until they had brought quite a significant amount of land under the plough.

They avoided the valley bottom which was too swampy and the highest escarpments which were not sufficiently sheltered.

Government

One of the greatest contributions made by the Anglo-Saxons and the Danes, was the idea of Government by Consent.

Their leaders were not originally kings but Elder Men who could only govern with the consent of the Witan or council. They met on a rounded hill high above the Spen River and they called this the Hustings Knowle. At their great Council which was held in the open air, they elected their chiefs, passed laws and discussed public affairs.

We get the word Hustings from this, where the election of Members of Parliament are proposed. Hus means house and a Thing was a meeting place. The word Tin, Ting or Thinge derives from the Norse Tinga which means to speak.

One of the most significant functions of the meetings was the administration of justice.

A circle was made from hazel twigs or upright stones. In the centre of the circle stood the Bloodstone (Blottstein). This was a huge stone with a sharp ridge on which the backs of criminals condemned to death, were broken. Each of the three presidents of the leading man would appoint twelve Dooms Men to sit with him in the circle.

This became a court of justice with three judges and thirty-six jurymen inside the circle, watched by the ordinary people outside it.

So this Knowle of land was the centre of things and it seems appropriate therefore that down the centuries an important building should occupy this spot; Liversedge Parish Church.

And of course the street name Knowler Hill also reminds us of those early inhabitants and how this knoll or hill was the gathering place for the whole valley.

Meetings continued here from the 7th Century onwards and a Manorial Court was still held here during the late Middle Ages.

There were at the time, three pathways approaching the hill; one from Littletown, one from Hightown and one from Heckmondwike.

Religion

The Anglo-Saxons were Pagans but they were gradually converted to Christianity after the Pope sent St. Augustine to the country, in 597.

It was a hard task for the missionaries, especially in the North, but by the 7th Century, there was an English Church and churches and monasteries began appearing.

At first, Christians would worship in the open air. Preaching crosses would be erected. Later, a wooden church with a thatched roof would be built to shelter the worshippers.

When the Pagan Vikings attacked; King Alfred, the King of Wessex, was involved in a battle for survival for Christian England and his victory marked the start of an England united by language and religion.

The country had, at first, been split into many Anglo-Saxon Kingdoms but in the 9th Century with the increasing threat from the Vikings, Alfred's grandson Athelstan was recognised as the first King to rule over the whole of England. He adopted the title Rex Anglonum Saxonum.

People began to think of themselves as English. And churches assumed an important role in unifying the country.

There were three Saxon churches built to serve the growing villages and hamlets of the Spen Valley. These were Hartshead Church, Birstall Church and Whitechapel, the Chapel of Ease belonging to the Birstall Parish.

St Peter's Church Hartshead

This is situated outside the village of Hartshead which suggests it was built to serve the whole surrounding area. It was built at the highest part of the escarpment.

Reminders of the Saxon Church are the base of the font within the church and the stump of an old yew tree in the churchyard, which was possibly planted at the consecration of the original wooden church. This is quite an extraordinary relic from Saxon times.

Hartshead Church was part of the Parish of Dewsbury.

The rest of the Spen Valley had its Parish at St Peter's in Birstall which also dates back to Saxon times.

St Peter's Church Hartshead on the site of the Saxon Church built of wood, with the remains of the 900 year old Yew Tree

St Peter's Church Birstall

This was by far the most important church in the whole region. Its parish stretched from Bradford in the west, to Dewsbury in the east.

Missionaries came from the new church at Dewsbury and a preaching cross was erected followed by a small church built of wood. This was to be the church by the Burg-steall, Birstall Church. So the settlement took its name from the Church.

The base of the cross now sheltering inside the church has already been described. But there is one more relic from the Saxons within the church and this is a decorated grave slab.

These relics show that Birstall was a Christian site before 1066.

St Peter's Church Birstall on the site of the original Saxon Church

The Chapel of Ease at Whitechapel

There was a wooden church here in Anglo Saxon times. It was simply called Heaton Chapel at this time. It was built so that people living in the area of Cleckheaton, Scholes, Oakenshaw and Wyke did not have to travel all the way to Birstall every Sunday.

Many Parish Churches had to build these little chapels in the days when the parishes were very large and consequently villagers had to walk long distances. They were allowed to use the chapels of ease for Sunday services but were compelled to use the main church at Birstall for baptism, wedding and funeral services.

The Chapel of Ease at Whitechapel on the site of the original wooden church from Saxon times

The People

And what about the people who worshipped at the churches and farmed the land. How do we find out about them?

One of the most informative and delightful books about the Spen Valley was written in 1893 by the Heckmondwike local historian Frank Peel. In common with similar historians up and down the country, he was wanting to document a way of life that had disappeared with the Industrial Revolution and he researched the history of the region with great care.

His book is called, 'Spen Valley Past and Present.'

He found that Liversedge, unlike most towns of the West Riding, had a truly ancient history and indeed was the main part of the Spen Valley under cultivation before the Norman Conquest.

There were two Saxon Thanes owning the land. They were Levenot and Gerneber. Levenot was very wealthy, owning land in Thornhill, Whitley, Mirfield and Hartshead. Gerneber was also very rich.

There were also two Saxons holding land in Gomersal; Dunstan and Gamel. Dunstan was the more affluent of the two and he owned a house in York. His land extended to Batley, Morley, Cleckheaton and Pudsey. They were all patrons of St Peter's Church in Birstall.

These landowners farmed their land using the Open Field system of farming, where there were no hedges or walls and the fields were separated by strips of un-ploughed turf or Green Lanes. Each strip was a Furrow, or furlong, in length which was the length run by the plough before the horse turned around. The strips were shared out between the villagers. Under the Saxons, the Spen Valley was cultivated and flourishing.

Apart from the the names of the landowners however, we don't know much about the villagers themselves.

CHAPTER 3: THE LATER MIDDLE AGES: 1066 - 1500

THE NORMAN CONQUEST 1066

There were more Viking invasions at the end of the 10th Century and then, in January 1066, there were three rival claimants for the throne of England on the death of Edward the Confessor, the Saxon King.

The heir to the throne was Harold Godwinson. He was a Saxon. There was also a Viking; King of Norway, by the name of Harald Hardrada. And finally there was William, Duke of Normandy, who claimed he had an agreement with Harold Godwinson that he would be the next King. (It so happened that Harold had given this promise when he was William's prisoner).

Harold Godwinson saw off his Norwegian rival, Harald Hardrada, at the Battle of Stamford Bridge but was defeated and killed at the Battle of Hastings by Duke William. William was crowned William I, King of England, on Christmas Day 1066 after a momentous year in English History!

William the Conqueror's invasion was to become the last of the invasions of the Middle Ages and it left its mark in the Spen Valley, as throughout the land.

THE DOMESDAY BOOK 1086

At first the North of England remained free under a Saxon called Morcar but then he began to be too independent.

So, William I sent one of his Normans to take over. This man was so cruel that the men of Yorkshire rose up against him, destroying his troops. William was incensed by this uprising and he vowed to destroy these people together with, *'Whatever supported human life.'*

Historians agree that thousands of people died in what can only be described as a massacre.

How thoroughly William wreaked his vengeance can be seen twenty years later because that was when he had his land and property documented in the Domesday Book, in 1086. Over and over again is the description, *'..it is waste.'*

These are some extracts, *'In Heton (Cleckheaton) Dunstan and Ravenhil had six carucates of land to be taxed, where there may be three ploughs. Ilbert has it and it is waste.'*

Scholes is not mentioned so we can assume that this, like Cleckheaton, was 'waste'.

'In Wiche (Wyke), Stainhulf and Westre had four carucates of land to be taxed, where there may be two ploughs. Ilbert has it and it is waste.'

'In Gomersal, Dunstan and Gamel had four carucates of land to be taxed, where there may be six ploughs. Ilbert has it and it is waste.'

Heckmondwike is not mentioned but it was included in the manor of Gomersal. All the villages were depopulated and all were described as, *'et vastum est.'*

All except Liversedge, *'In Liversec, Levenot and Gerneber had four carucates of land to be taxed where there may be two ploughs. Now Raidulf has it of Ilbert.'*

This Ilbert was Ilbert de Lacy, one of the Normans who had come to England with William and he was the new master of this part of Yorkshire with his castle at Pontefract. He also built a small castle on Castle Hill near Huddersfield. This castle is mentioned in a charter of King Stephen to Henry de Lacy in the 1140's. It took 250 years for the land to recover and be brought back into cultivation. Liversedge however had escaped and as the Domesday Book tells us, it was divided into two Manors or villages, separated by Clough Beck, a tributary of the Spen river. These manors were in the hands of two men; Raidulf and Levenot.

Raidulf had the manor on the Roberttown side of the beck and Levenot lived on the Hightown side. Raidulf was the heir of Gerneber. He had a house near to the present Liversedge Hall (possibly on the present site).

Levenot's house was in Hightown. We don't know exactly where this was but there is evidence of an important building called Liversedge Place. This was very probably on the site of Haigh House on Halifax Road because it stood near to the centre of the village. There would also be a Pinfold there for stray sheep.

We don't know much about Levenot but we know that Raidulf lived in some style at Liversedge Hall. Surrounding the hall would be the Inland where the slaves lived in little huts and then the Outland was where the open fields stretched. Beyond these were the Commons where the cattle roamed and also woodland running down to the Spen Valley where the pigs were driven to feed.

The other great manor, after 1066, was that of Gomersal which included Birstall and Heckmondwike.

This was in the hands of a Norman family called the Tillys. Hugh de Tilly was given the land by Ilbert de Lacy. It is possible that their manor house was at Oakwell. Certainly there was a settlement near the site of Oakwell Hall dating to the time of the Tillys. This was a very large manor and the seat of it was in close proximity to the (new) St Peter's Church and to a corn mill built on the banks of Birstall beck.

THE FEUDAL SYSTEM

These manors were part of the feudal system which, along with the building of Motte and Bailey castles throughout the land, were meant to allow the King to keep firm control over his new country so that he could spend much of his time in his French dukedom.

The Lords of the Manor only leased their land from the King.

Norman nobles like Ilbert de Lacy leased the land from the King and they in their turn leased land to the Lords of the Manors like the Tillys of Oakwell, and Levenot of Liversedge Place and Raidulf of Liversedge Hall.

The labourers for the Lords of the Manors were the Bordars who had to perform services for the Lord and supply him with goods like poultry and other provisions. Some bordars were carpenters, others smiths and masons. But all worked for the benefit of their master.

The lowest class of labourers were the Villeins. They were slaves and could be bought and sold. They did the heavy work like hedging and ditching. At certain times of the year, the Lord of the Manor held a feast. This would be at Christmas, Easter, harvest time and after the ploughing ended in spring and autumn.

The usual diet of the labourers would be unleavened bread and cheese and bacon. Milk would be drunk in summer and water in winter. Richer people drank beer and ate mutton, pork and beef. The feudal system continued throughout the next three centuries.

THE POLL TAX

The returns of the Poll Tax of 1379 (after the Domesday Book our most helpful yardstick) shows that Liversedge inhabitants had to pay far more than Gomersal, Cleckheaton and Heckmondwike. Liversedge was the most populous and important of the villages and paid a total of £29.

The Pound was the unit of account from Anglo-Saxon days. It was equal to 240 silver pennies which weighed one pound of silver. The Penny became the standard coin of England (but it was gradually reduced in weight and by Tudor times it was debased and mixed with copper).

The Poll Tax was intended to pay for the war being waged against France and its ally Scotland. A Groat was to be paid by everyone over the age of sixteen. Wealthy folk paid more.

In the Middle Ages the name groat was given to thick silver coins as opposed to the thinner silver pennies. They were worth four times more.

The records gives us the names of those paying the tax so it's almost like a Census. These names also give a clue as to the occupations of some individuals. The name Walker is evidence that cloth was being produced as this indicates the Fulling of cloth. This name occurs in Liversedge. There is no sign that cloth was being made in Cleckheaton but various trades are represented there by the names Robert de Mylner, Thomas de Mason and Robert de Naylor.

The Heckmondwike surnames also involve trades. There are Wrights, Lysters, Mylners and Tynkelers. Some of the oldest Heckmondwike families can be traced back to the Poll Tax; the Cokes (which would become Cook), the Rhodes, the Popplewells and the Listers. The inhabitants of Stubley Farm were also mentioned as paying Poll Tax.

It is interesting to see that the Spen Valley was not unimportant in 1379. By comparison, Huddersfield raised only 19 shillings, Halifax 12 shillings and Bradford 23 shillings. The great centres of population in the Middle Ages were Doncaster, Selby, Pontefract and Wakefield.

The Poll Tax does show however, that the majority were not wealthy enough to pay more than a groat. Most people lived in houses built from wattle and daub and without windows and chimneys. The fire would be in the middle of an earthen floor and animals would share this one open space.

Filthy conditions led to deadly epidemics which swept through the manors. In 1390-91 Yorkshire suffered its own Black Death which wiped out a third of the population.

So the Poll Tax, like the Domesday Book, enable us to take a peep behind the scenes of the Spen Valley all those centuries ago. We can now take a closer look at each manor from the 12th to the 15th Century.

THE MANORS

LIVERSEDGE

Liversedge was still divided into two manors.

There was Liversedge Essolf centred round the house called Liversedge Place in Hightown and this manor stretched along the ridge of land to the north of Clough Beck.

Liversedge Robert, taking its name from Robert de Flamburgh (a descendant of Gerneber) lay south of the beck and was made up of present day Roberttown and Norristhorpe. Liversedge Robert stretched along another ridge of high land. These escarpments were much better for farming than the low lying swampy valley below.

Norristhorpe developed much later, from the area around the manor house, and also the corn mill; hence the place names we have today such as Liversedge Hall Lane, Cornmill Lane and Millstone Rise. Norristhorpe was often nicknamed Doggus because of the fact that the Lord's hounds were kenneled there.

Liversedge Essolf

Essolf was Lord of Great and Little Liversedge which became known as Hightown, Littletown, Millbridge and Flush. At first he was the more important of the two Liversedge Lords. He was immensely wealthy. His home, Liversedge Place, on the site of the present day Haigh House, was the centre of the manor and nearby was the village green and the pinfold.

It appears though, that Essolf did not remain a wealthy man because, not only did he divide his possessions between his eight sons, but he was also a strong sympathiser of the crusading knights in their struggle against the Turks and so he gave generously to the knights of St John of Jerusalem; the Knights Hospitallers.

An interesting reminder of the Knights Hospitallers still exists in Hightown.

A religious symbol of the time was a pair of crossed keys and an inn by the name of The Cross Keys has stood on Halifax Road for centuries. The original inn may have been a hospice built by the Knights Hospitallers to provide food and accommodation for travellers.

When he died in 1165, Essolf left no great property but his sons were all well-off landowners. This support for the Crusades continued down the generations as the Liversedges of Liversedge Essolf gave liberally to the cause.

Gradually their wealth was depleted and over the following generations, the members of this family became anonymous Yeomen. However we do know something about them from the Hanson Papers.

In 1893, Frank Peel, the Heckmondwike historian already mentioned, discovered among manuscripts preserved at the Bodlean Library in Oxford, a number of papers written by a man named John Hanson.

John Hanson had married the heiress of the Liversedge Essolf family in the reign of Elizabeth I.

He found that a Peter de Liversedge had married, in 1265, the heiress of Robert de Liversedge. She was called Isandra. Their son, Thomas, inherited Liversedge Place but over the years the name disappeared and reappeared when the land changed hands.

By 1409, one of the de Liversedges, a man called Robert who happened to be the vicar of Birstall Church, did his best to restore the family fortunes by buying back some of the ancestral lands.

Then in just two years, this property, so carefully accumulated, was squandered and Alice, the heiress of the de Liversedges married into a new family which now took precedence in this area; the Rayner family.

Liversedge Robert

The family of Liversedge Robert, living at Liversedge Hall, were not as generous as the Lord of Liversedge Essolf.

In fact they kept all their ancestral land and were always looking for opportunities to expand their estate.

Present Day Liversedge Hall on the site of the medieval hall.

By 1280, Sir Robert de Liversedge was living in considerable state. However, his only heir was a daughter named Isola. In 1320 she married Sir Edmund Neville, a Lancashire knight. So the Liversedge Robert estate passed into the hands of one of the largest aristocratic families in the land.

This is why the history of Liversedge is such an interesting one, being played out on the national and even international stage.

The Nevilles were themselves descended from the Saxons, not the Normans. They were connected by marriage to most of the influential families in the land and because they were a capable lot, their services were in demand from a succession of Monarchs; usually holding high offices of state. In 1320, the first Neville was duly certified as the Lord of the township of Liversedge. He was also an MP for Lancaster.

In 1322 he helped King Edward I drive out the invading Scots who had got so far south that they were wintering at Morley! He was given, as his reward, a grant of Free Warren at Liversedge, which meant he could hunt in his own and his neighbours land quite freely. His grandson, another Sir John, became Sheriff of Yorkshire.

Around 1450, a great Baronial hall was built with battlements and mullioned windows. In the west wing was a chapel where marriages would be celebrated. The hall was at the top of a ravine and surrounded by a park. Frank Peel described it as a, 'noble residence.'

Their park is remembered today in the names, Park Farm and Lodge Farm. The Nevilles remained among the most important West Riding Gentry for the next 250 years.

CLECKHEATON

At the beginning of 1254, the manor of Cleckheaton was held by the Norman knight Sir John de Longvilliers but in that year he lost his life while serving with English forces in Gascony and he left his land to his infant daughter, Margaret. His death led to an enquiry to ascertain the extent of his estates and the report gives us a detailed description of Cleckheaton at that time.

It tells us that it was divided into two parts, Heaton (Cleckheaton) and Akenscale (Oakenshaw and Scholes). It describes the Bondmen and the conditions under which they lived. They were slaves and each man held a Bovate of land, 12 acres of strips scattered through the arable fields.

Each had rights to graze animals in the meadows and common pasture. Each had a single storey timber framed cottage with a Toft and Croft. The toft was the area of the cottage with sheds for cattle and a vegetable garden. The croft was the grazing area nearby.

The bondmen had to pay money to the Lord and they had to carry out services and work for him. They also had to pay a Merchet if a daughter was to be married and a Lecherwyt if a daughter lost her honour!

A document of 1365 tells us something more. In that year a grant was made to William of Mirfield of lands in the manor of Cleckheaton. He was buying the land and the bondmen themselves with all their families and possessions. So bondmen could be bought and sold with the land.

There were a few Freemen and they could sell their land and move elsewhere. But they too had obligations. They had to serve with the King's army at home or abroad.

By the end of the 14th Century, Cleckheaton had developed into a small community of about a hundred people. They probably occupied the site of the present town centre on a terrace above the River Spen. The settlement was situated between two lanes. Tofts Lane (now known as Northgate) separated the cottages from the open fields to the west, and Hunsworth Moor Lane (now called Bradford Road) separated the cottages from the open fields leading down to the river.

Crops were grown in six large open fields around the village. Each field was about 25 acres in size and was divided into strips so that each farmer had strips in each field. Some of the field names can still be recognised in street names today. Names such as Upper White Cliff, Chairbarrows, Peaselands, the Tofts and Townsteads. These fields stretched westwards towards Scholes and eastwards as far as the River Spen.

In addition to the fields there were two areas of open pasture at the Green and Hunsworth Moor.

Behind the open fields was a wide expanse of uncultivated wasteland, Cleckheaton Common. Every villager had the right to graze their sheep and cattle on the common.

Farming was organised so that each villager shared an equal responsibility to work together in the fields, growing the same crop. This meant that one field was left fallow for a whole year to rest. This method of crop rotation was essential before the days of fertilizers.

The villagers did not own the land. They paid rent to the Lord of the Manor and were obliged to work on his land.

As at Liversedge, this was Ilbert de Lacy at first and then a branch of the Neville Family and by the end of the Middle Ages, the Danby family.

Scholes

The village of Scholes had three large open fields. Present day names give us a clue as to where they were: Westfield; between Westfield Lane and Wyke, Northfield; between Whitechapel Road and Whitehall Road, and Oldfield; between the village and Halifax road. There was also pasture land between the west and north fields for grazing animals.

Another area of pasture was Well Lands (Wellands Lane area). The Tofts and Crofts and the village Green would be on the present day centre of Scholes. The commons were to the west of Oldfield and the Moor was between Scholes and Moorside Road and Moorbottom. Both commons and moor had their uses. They produced peat for firing and extra grazing for sheep, cattle, ponies and donkeys. The area of present day Scholes has not altered much since the middle ages.

Oakenshaw:

Oakenshaw was also a part of Cleckheaton but this was not yet a village, just a scattering of small farmsteads.

THE MANOR OF GOMERSAL

From the Norman Conquest, throughout the Middle Ages, Heckmondwike was part of the very large manor of Gomersal. Gomersal and Liversedge were the two oldest villages in the area. Liversedge spanned the ridges and valleys south of the Spen and Gomersal covered the slopes of the escarpment north of the Spen.

The manor of Gomersal stretched from the banks of the Spen where the tiny hamlet of Spen grew around a corn mill and up the lane, Spen Lane, as far as Gomersal village itself clustered around the top of the hill, Hill Top and along the ridge to Moor Lane on the edge of the uncultivated moorland. It then stretched down to the tiny hamlet which had developed around St Peter's Church at Birstall with its own corn mill.

To the east of Spen Lane was another hamlet, Little Gomersal and then the hamlet of Popeley and beyond that the village of Heckmondwike. The fields between Gomersal and the hamlet of Birstall were the Glebe lands. Across the valley of Birstall Beck was the seat of the Lord of the Manor, at Oakwell. The earliest record of the people who lived here is in 1150 when the Norman Ilbert de Lacy granted Gomersal to Hugh de Tilly, and the vicar of St Peter's Church was Richard de Birstall.

The Hamlet of Birstall

In 1286, the Tillys gave their right of patronage in the church to the monks of Nostell Priory and in 1300, they gave them all their rights in the Rectory and the glebe lands which was all the land owned by the church. They also gave them the corn mill and mill pool near the church.

The loss of the corn mill was very hard on those living in most parts of the manor as they had now to walk all the way to the corn mill at Spen near to the boundary with Heaton (Cleckheaton) in order to grind their corn. (But for the Tilleys they had an easier passage to heaven as the monks were praying for their souls!

26

Nostell Priory now had considerable influence and the land they controlled was called Monk Ings, the monks fields. A name familiar today.

There would probably have been an inn on a site where (or near) The Black Bull is today, on Kirk-gate (which means the road leading to the church). This would have been very necessary because parishioners had to travel such a long way. There would also have been quite a collection of houses for the vicar and chaplains and their servants nearby.

Oakwell

Oakwell was the seat of the Lords of the Manor of Gomersal for 600 years.

This meant that it was the administrative centre; the Manorial Court was held there and it was a busy place because the Lord of the Manor was the largest landowner of the area. Excavations have shown that there was likely to have been a large collection of buildings, one being quite large, from the 13th Century. Two of the timbers found in the present building are early 13th Century.

The manor of Gomersal remained in the hands of the Tilly family throughout the 12th and 13th Centuries. It was Robert Tilly who got permission from King Edward I to give the church patronage to Nostell Priory.

In the 14th Century, the Tilly line died out and passed to the female line. Joan de Tilly married Roger de Leeds and so the Leeds family inherited the manor which by this time had mention of coal and iron workings and associated smithies which were on the commons of Birstall. One of these must have been at Birstall Smithies.

By the 15th Century, William de Leeds owned Birkenshaw, Popeley, Spen and Heckmondwike, as well as Gomersal, but as he died childless in 1433, his estates passed to his nephew, Ranulf Pygot and the manor passed into an even bigger estate.

In the middle of the century, the old manor house was replaced with a new building which was still made of timber but much larger and which occupied the site of the present Oakwell Hall.

Gomersal Village

The settlement of Gomersal village consisted of a line of cottages with their crofts along the top of the ridge, but without a real nucleus.

The open fields stretched beyond. There was one west of Latham Lane stretching as far as the hamlet of Drub. There was Gomersal field leading down to Oakwell. North of the village was moorland (Moor Lane area) and to the east lay the church glebe lands around Church Wood, Church Meadows, Monks Ings and Kirkgate leading to St Peter's Church.

Little Gomersal

Little Gomersal, by contrast, had a village green, surrounded by cottages and beyond were the the open fields and moorland used for common pasture.

By the 15th Century, the most important family was the Gomersall family who, despite their importance, were still tenants of the Lord of the Manor. Their estate appears to have stretched right down to Littletown. It is very likely that a prominent house stood on the site of the present Gomersal House.

Heckmondwike

During medieval times, the population of Heckmondwike was very small.

The Poll Tax of 1379 records there being only seven families, so perhaps 35 to 40 people. They lived in small isolated farmsteads such as Stubley Farm which dates from this period. These farms would be on high ground away from the marshy valley.

Their inhabitants would be self sufficient, producing just enough food for themselves and they would weave cloth for their own needs. There are records of weaving in Heckmondwike as early as the 13th century, when both weaving and fulling were apparently taking place at Stubley Farm.

There were certainly Walking or Fulling mills by 1350 as well as Dyeing using water from the Spen. The surname Lister was given to the dyers of Heckmondwike.

The Hamlet of Spen

In the 13th Century, John de la Spen owned the land and his homestead would probably have been where Spen Hall now stands. There was also, significantly, a Mill House.

The cornmill and the homestead would have been the next most important buildings. The common pasture was in the area that now forms the grounds of Spen House, (on the other side of the road from Spen Hall).

By 1316, there is a record of the land being given to Sir John de Thornhill and by then the hamlet covered the north bank of the Spen River; about 60 acres. In 1342, Sir John granted the land to John de Tilly, Lord of Oakwell Hall and thus the hamlet became part of the Oakwell estate.

Interestingly, this might well have been the only stretch of the river to be called Spen (after the hamlet it flowed through).

Streams and becks of this size tended to take the name of the places they passed through. So this stream starts as Hunsworth Beck and then becomes Spen Beck and later Marsh Beck then Rawfolds Beck and so on to the River Calder.

It was only in the 1860's that the name Spen was adopted for the whole 9 mile length. These villages and hamlets were the sum of the Manor of Gomersal.

Popeley

In the 14th Century, there was an imposing house near the site of the present Popeley Farm.

From the 12th Century, to the 14th Century, the Popeley family were prominent farmers and they held their land, all 80 acres, by their own right and not as tenants of the Lord of the Manor at Oakwell. This made them the second largest landowner in Gomersal.

This land had been bought by William de Popeley from Thomas de Birstal in 1373. Witnesses to this transaction were Roger de Ledes, John Neville and John de Stubley (from the neighbouring farm). Willelmus de Popeley was so rich by the time of the Poll Tax of 1379 that he was charged the maximum tax.

In the 15th Century, Richard de Popeley was under age when he inherited the estate and had to have two trustees.

These were the two most important men of Gomersal, the Vicar of St Peter's (who at this time was one of the de Liversedge family) and the Lord of the Manor, William de Ledes who was rather unscrupulous.

For example, he raised the taxes and rents on the two large houses owned by the Popeleys; at the Rydings, near Birstall and at Castle Hill near Little Gomersal.

When Richard finally took care of his inheritance, he went on to increase his possessions and in 1432, he held a prestigious position at Pontefract castle. At this time, two distinct lines of the Popeley Family emerged; one in Gomersal and the other one in Woolley, near Wakefield.

By the end of the 15th century, the Gomersal Popeleys were rich enough to have a stained glass window put into Birstall Church, complete with their family crest.

RELIGION IN THE MIDDLE AGES

The Domesday Book doesn't mention churches but we have written evidence to show the continued development of the three churches that the Saxons had built of wood. The Normans re-built each of them in stone. They had stone floors with rush matting and no seats

St Peter's Hartshead

This church was re-built about 1120. The only Norman remains are the south doorway with its tell-tale rounded arch and zig-zag pattern and the Chancel arch with zig-zags and lattice patterns etched into the stone and also the remains of a Norman pillar supporting the font.

The church would have solid stone pillars but no tower. A tower was probably added when the church was re-built about 1350, when a Tithe Barn was also constructed.

Chancel arch, St Peter's, Hartshead

The base of the of the font; St Peter's, Hartshead

Across the road from the church were a Mounting Block and the village Stocks (always found near to a church).

Village Stocks, Hartshead

One other intriguing relic as we have seen already, is the trunk of a yew tree in the graveyard. Yew was planted at the time of the consecration of a church so this was possibly planted in medieval times.

Legend has it that Robin Hood used wood from this tree to shape arrows for his famous bow.

Whitechapel

This was re-built between 1130 and 1150. Primary evidence here is the Norman font and also a tombstone belonging to a crusading Knight. The font has interesting carvings which involve Celtic fertility figures.

This was the Chapel of Ease for Birstall Church and served the needs of those living too far away from Birstall to travel. It was still called Heaton Chapel and it now had the right of Baptism as well as Sunday services, and ensured, *'That no man would die without Baptism.'*

St Peter's Birstall

This was re-built during the first half of the 12th Century. It was a small sandstone building with a square tower which had narrow windows and a spiral staircase which can still be seen today.

The building was narrow, only the same width as the tower, the lower part of which still survives. It would have small unglazed windows and would have looked rather like a barn.

Important evidence from this church includes some 12th Century grave covers decorated with Norman chevron patterns and a Norman font. This latter is a very plain structure with a tagellated decoration around the base but it is a very important monument.

It shows how Birstall was the centre for baptisms. St Peter's Church, Birstall, continued to be the focus of religious activity for the whole area.

As we have already seen, in 1286 the Parish of Birstall became involved with the Augustinian Priory at Nostell. Robert de Tilly, Lord of the Manor of Gomersal, gave the Advowson of the church so that the monks would pray for himself and his family and ensure a speedy access to Heaven.

The monks had the right to choose the vicars and they looked after the chancel part of the church.

The church was enlarged in 1200 and then in 1320.

There are still fragments of stone from these churches. But the most interesting relics are three stone burial slabs believed to belong to the Knights Hospitallers who owned land in the parish.

These are possibly from the 13th Century. The carved chalice on one of these suggests that the man buried under this stone was a priest and not a lay member.

Stone burial slabs, St Peter's, Birstall

Between 1490 and 1520 the church was re-built and the tower was extended by another floor and a belfry. Relics from this church are the octagonal font and several darkly stained wooden pew ends.

Some of these show family heraldic devices and some have pictures showing the tools of family trades; for example a mason's square and a pair of compasses and one has a woolcropper's shears and a teasel.

Wooden pew ends, St Peter's, Birstall

A hamlet grew around the church. There were several chaplains working in the parish and their homes and the Rectory were right next to the church.

The other important building was The Black Bull Inn; very probably on the site of the 17th Century inn which still serves thirsty travellers today. In the Middle Ages this was an important resting place for parishioners who had travelled considerable distances.

THE ROLE OF THE CHURCH IN THE MIDDLE AGES

The church was very important in people's lives. It fulfilled many of the functions performed by local and national government today. To pay for this work, the church-goers had to pay a tenth of their income, or Tithes, to the church.

There would be a tithe barn next to each of the churches. These were to store the church Levy or tax, which was paid in crops and lesser tithes like eggs and honey.

Priests were more like business men and were very often guardians to those who had not come of age. Contracts were drawn up in the church grounds. Social life revolved around the church and plays and festivals were held there.

But perhaps the most interesting fact about all three churches is that they are all in outlying positions. Not one of them is the nucleus of a village. This resulted in some lack of control over the population by the priests who conducted their services every week but were unable to visit their huge parishes very easily.

In addition to the churches, there was one other religious establishment, which in the 20th Century, was to give its name to a large Metropolitan area, and that was Kirklees Priory.

KIRKLEES PRIORY AND THE STORY OF ROBIN HOOD

A small settlement in a little valley between Mirfield and Hartshead, was cleared in 1151 and a religious order called the Cistercians moved in and built a Priory.

It was founded by Reiner de Fleming, who lived at Hartshead Hall on Hartshead Hall Lane and who was Lord of the Manor of Hartshead and Clifton.

The church was quite small, only 80 feet by 20 feet, and the 40 foot cloisters were sited on the south of it. There was a dormitory along one wall of the cloister, over the parlour and the chapter house. The parlour had a chimney and two bay windows. On the first floor along the south side of the cloister, was the dining room and on the west side there were five small study rooms. The chaplain had his own house apart from the main building.

The Cistercian Order was very strict; no meat was eaten, no possessions were allowed and life was lived in a simple puritanical way. It was, however, a wealthy Order and held lands all over West Yorkshire, including Nun Ing, the name for 50 acres of land in Mirfield.

Cistercian priories like that at Kirklees, were numerous all over Europe but there were only thirty in England. They were usually small in size and never had more than 22 nuns.

These White Ladies, so called because of their white woollen tunics, were very often the unwanted daughters of the gentry and while at first they followed the strict rules, as time passed they became less dedicated.

They began to live quite worldly lives. In fact by 1315 there were scandalous reports of goings on at Kirklees. Alice de Raggid, together with Elizabeth de Hopton and Joan de Heton, were accused of admitting both clergy and laymen into the Priory!

The Priory carried with it the privilege of sanctuary. The Dumb Steeple close by, is supposed to be the Doom Steeple to which a man fleeing from justice, could come for safety. It is possible that Robin Hood came here for sanctuary as well as medicine from his kinswoman, the Prioress.

ROBIN HOOD

Of course it's difficult to prove the very existence of Robin Hood. He appears in ballads, poems and even official documents.

One such document, dating back to 1230, mentions a Robertus Hood, fugitivus in the financial accounts of a sheriff. There was also a Robert Hode who was given the King's pardon in 1328. This Robert came from Wadsley, a village near Sheffield and this was near the village of Loxley.

Lots of the ballads from the middle ages refer to him as Robin of Loxley and that he lived as an outlaw in the Forest of Barnsdale to the north of Doncaster. In fact it is the ballads which have inspired the myths and legends surrounding this man.

One the first ballads about Robin Hood was written by Piers Ploughman in 1377 but it is from two 15th Century ballads that we have the story of his death in the gatehouse of Kirklees Priory.

Early 16th Century gatehouse of Kirklees Priory on the site of the medieval gatehouse.

The poems tell us of Robin Hood travelling with Little John to Kirklees Priory; a priory noted for its riotous nuns, in order to be bled. This was a standard medical treatment for just about everything in the middle ages.

The story implies that the Prioress (who was his kinswoman) plotted to kill him, aided by Robin's enemy, the Earl of Doncaster.

In order to do this, she sent Little John away. She then opened up one of Robin's arteries so he would bleed to death. When he realised he was dying, he slew the treacherous Earl of Doncaster and with the strength in his body ebbing away, he summoned Little John by blowing three blasts on his hunting horn.

It was obviously too late but Little John helped him to fire his last arrow from the gatehouse window where he lay. He had asked Little John to bury him wherever the arrow fell. He also forbade his friend to punish the Prioress because it was the code of honour among chivalrous men in the middle ages, never to hurt a woman.

(And did that arrow come from the yew tree in Hartshead Churchyard?)

So this is the legend and there is a grave, but it is 650 yards away so he would have had to have been a superb archer to achieve that distance.

But allegedly he was just that. A brilliant archer.

The gravestone is in a secluded glade in a woodland area and bears the inscription, in Old English,

'Here underneed this laitle stean	*'Here underneath this little stone*
Laiz Robert Earl of Huntington	*Lies Robin Earl of Huntington*
Nea arcir ver as hei sa geud he	*No archer was there ever so good as he*
As piple kauld im Robin Heud	*And people called him Robin Hood*
Sick Utlawz as hi an iz men	*Such outlaws as he and his men*
Will England nivr si again'	*Will England never see again'*

Path leading to....

...Robin Hood's Grave, Kirklees Estate

So what is the truth?

It is possible that Robin Hood was killed at Kirklees Priory as it is only 10 miles away from Wakefield, an important town at that time. The ballad tells us that he was killed by a relative who was in charge of a Priory and that this was 22 years after he left the King's service in 1324. That means he would have died about 1346 and that is when Elizabeth de Stayton was Prioress and she was indeed, the cousin of Robin's wife, Mathilda. The story tells us that the Prioress took her own life and Elizabeth is recorded as dying in 1347.

When the present grave was excavated, nothing was found. The grave had in fact been moved at least three times. The original grave slab disappeared some time after 1665. So the mystery remains with us.

THE END OF THE MIDDLE AGES

By the end of the Middle Ages, the great de Lacy Estate, created at the Norman Conquest, was divided into several manors.

Gomersal, Heckmondwike and Birstall belonged to the de-Pygot Family of Oakwell Hall.

Hartshead-cum-Clifton belonged to the Flemyng Family of Hartshead Hall on Hartshead Lane. They also owned a hall on the site of the present Highley Hall in Clifton. They in turn leased their land from the de Warennes, the Lords of the great manor of Wakefield.

Liversedge Robert passed to the Nevilles of Liversedge Hall and Liversedge Essolf was not owned by any one family. It had been sub-divided over the years until the manor disappeared.

Hunsworth and East Bierley belonged to the vast estates of the Savile Family of Thornhill Hall, Dewsbury. This family was one of the most powerful and influential families in the whole of Yorkshire.

By the time of Sir John Savile's death in 1504, the family owned land throughout West Yorkshire and also land in Cheshire and Nottinghamshire. They were even related by marriage to King Henry VII.

The fact that the region was no longer in the hands of just one great land-owner however, played an important part in a growing political awareness in the minds of many farmers and tradesmen of the Spen Valley. The many minor Lords of the manor meant that there wasn't just one man in control of the whole area. This allowed for a climate of more freedom of expression.

Equally there was no single religious body to exercise control. The small Cistercian convent at Kirklees had little influence on the area as a whole. The Augustinian monks from Nostell Priory who owned church land at Birstall were usually un-interested in manorial or church business.

So there was no large religious body controlling the church in the middle ages. Moreover, the three churches were situated in outlying areas and this too led to a greater amount of independence in the Spen Valley.

Trade and industry did well because of the weakness of manorial control. Land was often divided between all the sons of a family not just the eldest, so farms became smaller and people had to supplement their income by producing cloth in their own homes and then selling it.

This encouraged the woollen industry to develop. Surnames started to emerge allied to the cloth trade, such as Lister (Dyer), Webster (Weaver) and Walker (Fuller). Some men became Clothiers, supplying wool to the cottagers to spin and weave into cloth and then collecting the finished cloth and taking it to market.

These clothiers became more prosperous and independent minded. They were less inclined to submit to the demands of the landlords. So in terms of trade, religion and manorial control, the people of the Spen Valley enjoyed more freedom than those in many other parts of the country.

CHAPTER 4: THE 16th CENTURY

RELIGION (The Reformation)

Until the 16th Century, the villages of the Spen Valley were relatively unaffected by national events. The Wars of the Roses passed them by, but the outcome of this particular civil war was the beginning of the Tudor Dynasty and the actions of the Tudor King, Henry VIII were to have a momentous impact here as in all parts of the land.

In 1534, the King divorced his wife, Queen Katherine, in order to marry Anne Boleyn. This led to the Pope excommunicating him. Henry retaliated by removing his kingdom from the Roman Catholic Church and forming his own Church of England with himself at the head.

All churches now had to adapt to these changes but the religious houses like monasteries and priories were to be closed down.

Kirklees Priory

By Tudor times there were only a few nuns at Kirklees Priory.

There was by that time however a good sized farm. One of the stone barns from the 15th Century, still survives today. The beams supporting it would probably have been from trees growing in the 1300's. This is an aisle barn with a stone floor for threshing. There is also a dovecote. The early 16th Century gatehouse may have been the farm manager's house. It has transomed windows on the first floor and is more like a home for the gentry.

The nuns were following a peaceful existence in their picturesque valley with their thriving farm when suddenly they were given notice to leave. In the event they were given 18 months reprieve and then the Priory was surrendered on 24th November 1539. Some of the nuns went to live in Mirfield. There were seven nuns listed on the Pension List.

The Prioress, Janet Kyppes received the biggest pension of 40 shillings. She is recorded as being buried in Mirfield Church in February 1562. One of the nuns, Isabel Rhodes had borne a child, so some of them were obviously still enjoying the worldly pleasures! Three more of the nuns, Celia Topcliffe, Joan Leventhorpe and Katherine Grace looked after an inn on the site of the former guest house of the Priory and called it The Three Nuns. This building stood on the car park of the present building, still called The Three Nuns.

A new family, the Armytages, bought the land belonging to the Priory in 1565 and they also bought the old Hartshead Hall, manor house of the Flemings, which they renovated and turned into a Dower House. Near the Priory ruins (and using stone from the Priory) they built for themselves a beautiful hall, Kirklees Hall. They also built a three storey malthouse with stone taken from the Priory.

Malthouse, Kirklees Hall Estate

The Armytages had been yeomen clothiers and they wanted the land here because of the water supply from the Nun Brook. Their cloth business flourished and they were able to buy their title. The head of the Armytage family kept strong links with Hartshead Church and was always the Lay Rector. It was his job to keep the church chancel in good repair.

Today there is still evidence of this link with Hartshead church. In the chancel (which survived the 1881 re-building) are the shields and memorials of the Armytage Family and there is a beautiful brass Coat of Arms set into the Chancel floor in what is the upper stone of the Armytage Family vault. In effect, the Armytage Family took over the role of medieval Lord of the Manor, having considerable land and farms and tenant farmers.

The estate was handed down through the centuries right up to 2008 when Lady Armytage died.

The Effects of the Reformation on the Three Churches

In 1546, the land at Birstall belonging to Nostell Priory was confiscated and given by Henry VIII to Trinity College Cambridge (names like Cambridge Road and College Street in Birstall come from this time). The relevance of this was that the glebe lands (church lands) were now leased out to wealthy laymen and the first of these was a man named Henry Batt.

From 1557, parish priests became known as Vicars and from 1558 churches had to keep a register of births, marriages and deaths. They also began keeping records of pews and their occupants and because these are described in reference to their position in the church, we can often find out about the social hierarchy of the congregation.

The churches of the area; Birstall, Hartshead and Whitechapel became Church of England. The agricultural population and the aristocracy still secretly followed the Roman Catholic faith but the increasing number of trades people were strongly Protestant (Church of England).

When Queen Elizabeth came to the throne in 1558, she was very tolerant about religion, but one event in her reign was to have cataclysmic results. And particularly in the manors of Liversedge Robert and Gomersal.

LIVERSEDGE ROBERT

The possessions of the Nevilles, Lords of the Manor of Liversedge, were continually increased over the generations by sensible marriage alliances.

Most Nevilles were Sheriffs of Yorkshire. The Baronial Hall, built in the 15th Century was very splendid with mullioned windows, lots of carved oak and a private chapel. It was surrounded by a well-wooded park stretching down the hillside to the River Spen.

The Nevilles continued to serve in the highest offices.

The Sir John Neville at the end of the 15th Century was a close friend of Richard Duke of Gloucester who later became King Richard III.

He was Constable of Pontefract Castle and this was perhaps the pinnacle of the Nevilles' fortune because when the King was killed at the Battle of Bosworth in 1485 during the Wars of the Roses, the Tudor Dynasty was established with Henry VII as King.

Now Sir John had to change his loyalties and he did manage to survive but it was not so easy when Henry VIII came to the throne and made the momentous decision to break with the Church of Rome.

Sir Robert Neville, the Head of the family at the time, totally opposed this but he used all his powers of diplomacy to save his estates from confiscation.

He avoided getting involved in the Pilgrimage of Grace in 1536 when there was a popular rising in Yorkshire against the religious changes. He died in 1540 and his eldest son yet another Sir John Neville took over the Manor.

Sir John, like much of the nobility and clergy of Yorkshire, outwardly supported the Reformation while secretly continuing to follow the Roman Catholic faith. Queen Elizabeth I was now on the throne and she was faced with threats of a Roman Catholic invasion from Spain as well as threats from English Roman Catholics who regarded Mary Queen of Scots (a devout Roman Catholic) as the rightful heir to the throne.

Finally, in 1569, Sir John Neville joined a conspiracy for displacing Queen Elizabeth and putting Mary Queen of Scots on the throne.

The Rising of the North was started by the Earl of Northumberland, but Sir John Neville was soon at the forefront of the rebellion.

The rebels were easily defeated by Elizabeth's armies and Northumberland and Neville fled to Scotland. Sir John was declared a traitor and all his possessions were confiscated by the Crown. His wife, Lady Neville and her ten children were turned out of the Hall which had been for three centuries the family seat.

It was reported in 1570 that Lady Neville, Sir John's wife, *'Is in a poor state, having only a white frieze gown and neither house, meat nor drink.'* She eventually joined her husband who had escaped to Spain and they settled there, living off a pension of £60 a year provide by the King of Spain (Elizabeth's arch-enemy).

After the disgrace of Sir John Neville, Queen Elizabeth leased the Manor of Liversedge to Edward Carey, a member of her Privy Council. He had the Queen's confidence and he and his three sons were all knighted.

It was one of these, Sir Robert Carey who rode his horse to Scotland in 1603, to inform King James VI that the Queen had died and that he, James, was now King James I of England. Under the Carey family, Liversedge was neglected and the tenants became increasingly impoverished. They were not used to an absentee landlord. Worse still, their rents were increased and times were hard.

47

GOMERSAL

We left the Manor of Oakwell in the hands of the Pygots.

They had been Lords of the Manor since 1433. But in 1512, the Lord of the Manor died leaving three daughters and no sons. So his estate was inherited by his daughter Joan who was married to Giles Hussey. She passed her lands on to her son Thomas Hussey.

Thomas Hussey was Lord of the Manor for just 6 months when, in 1565, he sold the entire estate to Henry Batt. The reason? Thomas Hussey was convicted of High Treason in 1569 for his part in the Rising of the North and he was imprisoned in the Tower of London.

So the two oldest manors of the area; Liversedge and Gomersal, lost their Lords as a result of their opposition to the Reformation.

Henry Batt

Henry Batt was one of a new breed of self made men with considerable land in Halifax already. His estate included Gomersal, Birstall, Birkenshaw, Spen, (Cleck)Heaton and Heckmondwike. He did not come from a noble family. He was one of the newly emerging Middle Class.

His chief ambition was making money. His tenants were expected to grind their corn at his cornmill (for a fee) and he insisted that this should still be done at Spen Mill and not Birstall Mill, making life difficult as the Spen Mill was far from the centre of the manor.

He was not liked and in fact he was well known for his unscrupulous behaviour! He stole the money intended for the building of a school. He took the Great Bell from the church belfry of St Peter's Church and sold it to another church. He stole from church funds and he even stole land from his wife Anne Popeley's family (he had married into the Popeley family to add gentrification to his line).

Henry Batt acted as business agent for the wealthy. These people had a high regard for his business abilities but did not consider him a social equal.

His son John Batt was a very similar character. In 1572 he enclosed the wastes and commons of Birstall which brought great hardship to the local people. However, as a result of an Inquiry into his father's malpractice, he had to compensate for all his wrongdoings.

He had the same energy and business acumen as his father however, continually building up his wealth and in 1583, he built the beautiful stone manor house which we see at Oakwell today. The central hall was used as a Manorial Courtroom.

The datestone can still be seen above the entrance with the initials JB - John Batt.

The Hamlet of Spen

Spen cornmill in the hamlet of Spen, was an important asset for the Lord of the Manor. Batt's tenants were still forced to use this and it made him a lot of money. Freemen could choose where they wanted to have their corn milled. There were several to choose from. The Cleckheaton Mill was at Blacup Beck; Millbridge Mill served Liversedge (plus one on the Cornmill Lane area) and Balme Mill served Hunsworth.

John Batt re-built Spen Hall at this time, on the medieval foundations. A wing of this house still remains.

THE RISE OF THE MIDDLE CLASSES

Men like Henry and John Batt were not born into aristocracy or gentry but were very ambitious and saw themselves as independent of any outside controls. They began buying land and building bigger houses, not high luxury but with separate rooms with fireplaces.

Another example of this new class of men was Thomas Taylor of Gomersal, who, in 1537 bought a house, garden and a croft. In 1550 he added to this the land behind his property which extended as far down as Fusden Lane and Cliffe Lane. This estate was called Lower Bawsons Cliffe.

In 1577 he was wealthy enough to add to this land yet again because Thomas Hussey was selling off manorial land to help pay off the fines incurred when he joined in the Northern Rebellion. By the end of the century, the Taylor estate included 30 acres of land.

Another family benefited from the sale of manorial land and that was the Norcliffe family who built a house on (or near) the site of Gomersal Hall.

These men came from humble beginnings but were able to establish themselves as a middle class with land and property. Others were smaller branches of old families like the Pygots.

Henry Pygot was Lord of the Manor of (Cleck)Heaton and Heckmondwike in Henry VIII's reign. His manorial seat was where Pynot Hall once stood and this name comes from Pygot.

CHANGES AT THE END OF THE 16th CENTURY

By the end of Tudor times, the main change had been the end of feudalism in Liversedge and Gomersal.

After the fall of the Nevilles and the Husseys and the disappearance of the Pygots, many people bought the freehold to the land they cultivated. They were now independent farmers. A new affluent middle class was emerging.

Spen Valley farmers were noted for their independence of mind. They doffed their caps to no - one and recognised no right in either squire or parson to question or meddle with them.

Another change was that farms were being built in outlying places as the Manorial System came to an end. These farms were often on land considered marginal for crops. This meant that farmers eked out a living by producing cloth as an additional source of income.

In Liversedge the old distinction between the two manors which had existed for hundreds of years, disappeared. This allowed the township to be organised on a community basis with new men who could come forward to take charge of local affairs. These men came from the ranks of the emerging middle classes.

Everywhere in the Spen Valley there was evidence of the development of the woollen industry as a cottage industry.

Every farmhouse had a loom on which the farmer and his sons wove cloth made from wool spun on the spinning wheels by the women of the family. Some of these families were becoming quite prosperous and able to make marriage alliances with the new middle class.

These well planned unions often brought with them extra land. An example of such a family was the Rayners, who steadily built up their fortunes in Liversedge.

LIVERSEDGE AND THE THE RAYNER FAMILY

The ancestors of this middle class family living in Liversedge, the Rayners, had actually arrived in England before the end of the 14th Century.

They were the descendants of the Flemish immigrants who were brought over by order of King Edward III to teach the English how to manufacture cloth, as opposed to sending wool to Flanders to be manufactured there.

The King had realised how wealthy Flanders had become as a result of their industry. The Flemish weavers settled first in Halifax and then in the Spen Valley.

One branch of the Raynor Family settled at Hare Park and one of their workshops was at the top of Hare Park Lane.

The origin of the word Hare Park is interesting. In the possession of Robert Rayner, we find a property with a Perocke, the old English word for park. And park simply meant an enclosure. It's possible that one of the early Rayners had an enclosed piece of land for small game such as hares at this place.

The Rayners gradually acquired land in the old township. For generations, they continued the manufacturing of cloth and farmed the land. Their estates were increased by the marriage of John Rayner to the heiress of William de Spen who owned lands down in the valley near Cleckheaton.

Another well planned union, in 1511 was between another John Rayner and the heiress to the old Liversedge Essolf family, a lady by the name of Alice. This gave the Rayners a bit of an aristocratic thread in their new family credentials and the young married couple settled in to Liversedge Place, the ancestral home. This medieval building must have been looking rather old by this time and in 1513, they had a new timber hall built.

Where is the proof of this?

In the 17th Century, Haigh House was built on this site; the large three gabled building we see today. This was built in stone and roofed with a King Post roof but there are survivals of John and Alice's house in this building. These relics from the early 16th Century timber-framed house are in the form of three timber roof trusses and other re-used timber.

The present owner has recently commissioned a tree ring analysis of this timber which has yielded some interesting facts.

The wood has been found to be locally grown oak. Moreover, the placing of the beams and trusses indicate that the original timber hall was an open hall of at least four bays.

A precise date was possible for the actual felling of the oak because freshly felled wood ('in the green') was nearly always used as standard practice. This oak was felled in the winter of 1512-1513 and the spring of 1513. The average age of the oak was 119 years so the oak trees were actually growing at the end of the 14th Century.

The date of the building of the hall ties in with the marriage of Alice de Liversedge and John Rayner.

The Rayner family continued their manufacturing and their farming until the end of the 16th Century when their fortunes declined.

But their story illustrates how one family could grow in importance because of their involvement in the cloth industry to such an extent that they could take over the estates of a once influential family.

The Organisation of Trades

Other trades developed apart from the cloth trade, for example Joiners, Masons, Tanners, Curriers and Shoemakers (Cordwainers). Trades tended to be carried on by generations of the same family as skills were taught from father to son.

In 1562, a formal set of rules was established where a Master Craftsman was allowed to employ young people in order to train them in a craft or trade. This education extended to social and business skills. These apprenticeships were set up between the young person's parents and a master craftsman.

An Indenture or legal agreement would be drawn up to set out the conditions. Apprenticeships usually started at the age of fourteen and the apprentice would not only work for the master in the family workshop, but would live with him as part of the family. Instead of being paid a wage he was fed and clothed and taught his trade. At the age of twenty-one, the apprentice would be allowed to leave and carry out the trade on his own.

CHAPTER 5: THE 17th CENTURY

LIVERSEDGE

In the reign of James I, Liversedge Robert was called Roberttown for the first time and Little Liversedge was known as Littletown. Also, papers from the time show that much of the wasteland had now become cultivated.

In 1615, Sir Philip Carey (Sir Edward's Carey's successor) started getting as much money as he could out of the manor so that he could live a rich lifestyle in his Somerset home. This included the raising of 'black diamonds.' The coal mines were first worked by the Careys. This mineral wealth encouraged him to buy even more of neighbouring localities which contained coalbeds.

Another way of increasing his wealth was to enclose some of the common land which encircled the township. This land was supposedly for the use of all, where families grazed their cattle, sheep and horses.

Now Sir Philip summoned the freeholders of the town to Liversedge Hall and persuaded them to divide this land between them, obviously at a good price to himself. These 456 acres were divided between 32 freeholders, who now became even richer.

Having sold off his lands, Sir Philip left Liversedge for good. The feudal way of life was over. The new men had taken over. These were the men who combined manufacturing with farming. The new Middle Class.

The history of the other part of the township of Liversedge is quite different.

The de Liversedge family had squandered its wealth and we left it at the point where the last heiress married into the Rayner Family. The very last time the mansion of the old Lords of Liversedge Essolf, Liversedge Place was mentioned, was in written evidence in 1608.

From the 17th Century, therefore, the name Liversedge included both the early manors and was in the hands of middle class families.

These men began taking over the work of organising local affairs. Now the most important family by far was the Greene Family.

The Greene Family

One of the free holders who took part in the arbitrary division of the common lands from Sir Philip Carey was John Greene, head of the family which was to occupy a prominent position in the Spen Valley for over a century.

There is a copy of a document drawn up in 1626, regarding a transaction between, *'John Greene, William Greene (his eldest son) Sir Philip Carey and Sir John Savile, regarding a messuage of twenty acres of land, five acres of meadow and twenty four acres of purchases in Liversedge.'*

John Greene, born in 1560, came to Liversedge from Ossett. He settled in Littletown and began manufacturing cloth from his farm there. He had seven sons; William, John, James, Richard, George, Thomas and Michael.

John Greene and his sons embarked on careers combining farming with cloth production and eventually succeeded the Rayners as the most important family in the Liversedge township, just as the Rayners had once stepped into the shoes of the de Liversedges.

They increased their wealth and importance throughout the 17th Century and this wealth was reflected in their grand houses, which included; Liversedge Hall, Castle House in Gomersal, Lowfold Hall and Duxbury Hall in Roberttown and the Rydings in Birstall.

There were several halls in Hightown, including Haigh House, Middle Hall and Lower Hall all on the main highway (Halifax Road) and Upper House on the site of present day Upper House Farm.

Even today there is evidence of this influential family because several of their fine houses still exist.

Middle Hall, Hightown, Liversedge

John Greene's eldest son was called William. He was a prosperous clothier and lived at Liversedge Hall. By the time that his own son John took over his business, England was involved in a Civil War.

The wealthy men of the valley; the Greenes, the Batts and the Armytages were supporters of the King when the Civil War broke out in 1642 between King Charles I, and his Parliament, led by Oliver Cromwell.

John Greene became Lieutenant of a regiment of foot under the command of Captain Batt.

Like his father William before him, John Greene lived at Liversedge Hall.

When he died in 1674, he was buried in the graveyard of Birstall Church. and a memorial was placed in the chapel which had been the former burial place of the Nevilles. The next few Greenes were buried here. This indicates a lot about their social standing.

William's second son (another William) was also very wealthy. He lived in Lower Hall in Hightown, after Liversedge Hall the grandest in the district. Built in the gothic style, it had a three-gabled frontage.

Lower Hall must have been a magnificent building. The grounds were entered by a great gateway set into a wall topped with heavy stone copings. There was a huge gothic archway and over the porch of the hall was a sundial, surrounded by an ornamental stone with the initials WMG 1666.

The village stocks were outside the gates of this Hall and though the building was demolished in 1939, the street name Lower Hall Lane, off Halifax Road and the base of the stocks (nearby a shop) remain. The village green and pond were once situated here.

William Greene too was a Royalist. His eldest son, William, inherited the house but his second son, Richard, built Lowfold Hall in Roberttown and carried on his trade as a clothier from there.

This beautiful house has been restored to something like its original grandeur. It still has the large workshop building nearby (which was always found next to the house of the clothier).

Both brothers served as Overseers of the Poor, showing their social status. They were now eligible to hold positions of importance in local government. Their work is documented in the Towns Books from the 1660's onwards. These were the books kept by the Parish Constables and Overseers of the Poor; in other words, the local officials of the time.

They tell of crimes committed, for example, the occasion when Richard Greene's workshop was broken into by robbers in 1689. There is also mention of how money was spent, so another item in the book is about the cost of erecting a maypole on the village green at Littletown. The local people may have been Puritans in their religious views, but after the restoration of Charles II, they were keen to get their maypole back so they could enjoy themselves!

The maintenance of law and order would certainly have been one of the main tasks of the constable and is probably the reason why the stocks were built in front of Squire Greene's house, Lower Hall. Stocks were usually placed near a church (as at Hartshead) but there was as yet no church in Liversedge.

So the Greenes, over the course of the century, came to hold much of the land and possessions and indeed the social status that had belonged to the De Liversedges in medieval times, and the Rayners in the 16th Century.

There were many other prominent clothiers at this time like the Oldroyds, the Pollards and the Kitsons but they, unlike the Greenes, all stood shoulder to shoulder with the Roundheads who were members of Parliament's armies.

In fact most of the middle class yeomen of the Spen were against the King. Fairfax and Cromwell found their most enthusiastic recruits among them. These men did not believe in fighting, but when they needed to stand up against what they considered to be an unjust monarch, they joined in the fierce fighting at Adwalton Moor and the siege of Thornhill Hall.

Some of them fought at Marston Moor. They then returned to their farms and no doubt grumbled about the Greene family and their support for King Charles.

Despite all of this, the Greene family did much to encourage the woollen industry of the Spen Valley.

CLECKHEATON

In 1650, the manor of Cleckheaton, Scholes and Oakenshaw was acquired by the Richardson family of Bierley Hall.

This was unusual because in most of the area, the Manorial System had died out. But the Richardson Family did not want to sell their land and break up their holdings.

In Liversedge, the open fields had been enclosed and divided into small compact holdings by the new commercial men who combined farming with cloth manufacture.

In Scholes too the arable farms were enclosed between 1622 and 1641.

In Cleckheaton however, the strong degree of manorial control held by the Richardsons (and the Savile Family who still owned Hunsworth) meant that the open fields; the Upper White Cliffe, the Lower White Cliffe, Peaselands, Townsteads, Chearbarrows and Tofts and the commons (Hunsworth Moor and Blacup Moor) and the Green (Upper and Lower Green) were not enclosed and the development of a cloth industry was retarded.

However, Card Setting was evident as early as the 17th Century and this was obviously the start of something special for Cleckheaton.

Master craftsmen were busy training apprentices in the art of Wire Drawing and Card Setting.

This would be carried on in the tiny settlement which had started to grow in the Middle Ages; between present day Northgate, which was then called Tofts Lane, leading straight on to open fields, in this case the Tofts Open Field and Hunsworth Moor Lane (present day Bradford Road), which led on to the open fields and meadows stretching down to the River Spen.

Oakenshaw remained a hamlet made up of scattered farms with some handloom weaving being carried out.

Market Cross, centre of the small hamlet of Oakenshaw

GOMERSAL

John Batt died in 1607 and his son Robert inherited the Manor but as he was a vicar in Wiltshire, the estate was managed by a cousin who lived in the Rectory house near the church.

His brother Richard lived at Spen Hall and collected the tithes as well as money from the cornmill.

When Robert died, his son John became Lord of the Manor. Whereas his grandfather and great-grandfather had been clever at making money, he was far better at spending it!

His main concern was living a lavish lifestyle. He was keen to mix with the neighbouring gentry. As part of this plan, he made dramatic improvements to his home, Oakwell Hall.

Oakwell Hall, Gomersal

At first there had been two storeys throughout the building but between 1630 and 1660, the chambers above the central hall were removed and the large mullioned window was put into the south wall and a gallery erected round the top of the stairs where a corridor had once been. These huge windows were fashionable at the time but this was by far the largest of its kind. The house was made even more luxurious by new plasterwork and painted paneling and fine furnishings.

John Batt was, by now, accepted by the gentry as more of a social equal. This meant that he could mix with the wealthy aristocratic families of Yorkshire.

One of John Batt's aristocratic friends was Sir William Savile of Thornhill Hall. In fact he was a Captain of the Company of the Militia Regiment of which Savile was the Colonel. From 1640 when war between the King and Parliament began to seem likely, Batt was often at Thornhill Hall, planning strategy.

In August 1642, John Batt saw action at Bradford and the following year in Leeds; both disasters. But in June 1643, his company, under the Earl of Newcastle, defeated the army of Sir Thomas Fairfax at the village of Adwalton, only a mile away from Oakwell Hall.

By 1644, however, the Parliamentarians were in control, following the decisive victory at Marston Moor and John Batt decided to give himself up so long as he didn't suffer physical harm! He did however incur a hefty fine; a tenth of the value of his property. To pay for this he had to mortgage some of his property and sell some of his land. John spent the rest of his life a broken man.

Financial problems dogged the next Lord of the manor; his son William and his son, another William. These money problems were added to by the fact that William's son John died childless and so by the end of the century, the Batt line disappeared. Yet another influential family fell into obscurity.

LITTLE GOMERSAL

The main family of this hamlet was still the Gomersall family and in the 16th Century they married into the Rayner family of Liversedge.

In 1619 the last of the line, John Gomersall, lived in a large timber house which is likely to be on the site of the present Gomersal House. He was a wealthy man owning over 150 acres of land to the south and west of the hamlet.

When the last male heir died, the female heiress, Elizabeth married into the Popeley Wentworth family and the estate stayed in their hands until 1833.

HECKMONDWIKE

By the 17th Century, woollen cloth production had become important enough to form the basis of a fairly prosperous local economy and the population increased to around 250 people living in 50 or more houses which occupied the area of the village green (the present park) and its surroundings. Some of these houses were larger and were built by the yeomen clothiers, the new middle class, for example Old Hall. But most were simple cottages.

THE COMMONS

Despite the enclosure of some of the commons by the Carey family, there were still large tracts of common land sweeping across from Gomersal right over towards Mirfield Moor. In parts they were merely a band and in other parts they were more extensive as over Hartshead Moor.

Peep Green Common started at the boundary of the Greene's farmland (by the Sepulchre) and stretched right down to the Armytage estate. In addition, the centres of Scholes, Cleckheaton and Heckmondwike all still had their common fields for grazing animals.

INCREASING POWER OF THE MIDDLE CLASSES

After the restoration of the Monarch, Charles II in 1660, the old Royalist gentry and indeed the Anglican Church, tried in vain to recover their position of authority. But the fines they had suffered under Oliver Cromwell had weakened them financially. Moreover, their income was static.

The clothiers by contrast were becoming ever more prosperous. They, like the Greene family of Liversedge, began to build fine houses and adopt a more luxurious lifestyle.

One of the beneficiaries of the transactions carried out as a result of John Batt's financial troubles, was Richard Peel of Gomersal who built Peel House in 1650. Peel was already a rich man by the middle of the 17th Century and his house was second only to Oakwell Hall in splendour. Like many, he had made his money by farming and cloth making.

Peel House, Gomersal

Another Gomersal beneficiary was Tempest Pollard who probably bought Pollard House from the Batts. Pollard benefited financially from his support of Parliament. The house was re-built in 1659 in a very grand style and according to the Hearth Tax of 1684 it had no less than nine hearths.

The Taylor family of Gomersal continued to build up their fortunes. In 1605 James Taylor had become rich enough to buy 30 acres of land where he built a house, outbuildings and garden. His son William continued in his father's footsteps as a yeoman farmer and clothier and by 1660, he was able to build a new house built of red brick.

This was quite rare and something of a luxury in an area where sandstone was plentiful. He also built a workshop where he could weave cloth. There was also a barn, a well, and a tentercroft. This was the start of a more elegant standard of living for the Taylor family in their Red House.

There are many other buildings from this time which show the prosperity of the middle class. Headlands Hall, in Liversedge, was built in 1690 by Joseph Farrer (but it has the remains of an earlier Tudor timber framed house.) Farrer was one of the early constables of Liversedge and the size of his house reflected this important position. His initials can still be seen above the front door of this splendid house: 'F' for Farrer and underneath the initials 'I' ('J') for Joseph and 'E' for Elizabeth his wife.

The beautiful medieval half-timbered Old Hall in Heckmondwike was enclosed in stone. It too was lived in by a Constable, John Keighley, uncle of Joseph Priestley. Swallows Nest was a large house built by Joseph Swallow, a dyer of Heckmondwike. Syke House was built by John Kitson of Cleckheaton.

The Armytage family of Kirklees Hall continued to prosper and they extended their home and their farm. A huge barn and a stable block were built when the Armytages started using horses for ploughing. The stable block has three storeys. The ground floor for the horses, the first floor for the hay and the top floor for the stable boys' living quarters.

Many of the stones on the Kirklees buildings have masons marks on them showing them to be from stones taken from the Priory.

This trend of building large houses in stone was becoming commonplace all over England as the middle classes grew in importance and we are fortunate that so many have survived in the Spen Valley.

There were also many smaller houses built for those involved in the cottage industry and some of these still stand, like the little group of cottages in Hartshead Lane. These are distinguished by the mullioned windows which allowed plenty of daylight into the upper rooms where the Looms were situated.

THE EFFECTS OF THE ENGLISH CIVIL WAR

The English Civil War was, without doubt, a major event affecting the lives of most families in the country and we have seen that Gomersal and Liversedge were particularly touched by it.

John Batt, John Greene and Sir John Armytage were prominent players. They raised their local troops when the Royal Order came to, *'Muster Your Militia.'*

Both King and Parliament mustered their troops in the area. Families were divided in their loyalties. And nearby Adwalton Moor was to be the battleground of a significant meeting of the two sides when the Royalists achieved one of their last victories in July 1643.

Perhaps the biggest effect of the war was the opening of the floodgates of Nonconformism with the execution of King Charles I. Religious rebels became known as Dissenters or Nonconformists. There were some really extreme groups and Oliver Cromwell had to try and curb these during the period that he governed England as a Republic. Most people in the Spen Valley found the Puritan religion of Cromwell more to their taste than the Anglican religion anyway.

They associated the Church of England, with the Monarchy and Authority in general. Religious dissent was another way of showing a need for more democratic, social and political ideas.

But when Charles II was restored to the throne in 1660, the Church of England was restored too. The King's government saw Nonconformist groups as a great threat and ordered them to disband.

Here in the Spen Valley, as in other parts of the country, people began to meet secretly in small groups in houses, farmhouses and inns. The laws against such meetings were strict and the Act of Uniformity said that all clergy had to use the Book of Common Prayer and that people had to worship in the established churches. If they refused, they couldn't hold any local office, they couldn't go to University and they couldn't even be buried in a churchyard.

The trouble was that people now felt they were fighting for their freedom. They had tasted religious freedom under Cromwell and they carried on meeting in secret. Nonconformism flourished and the Spen Valley was one of the strongest areas of dissent in the whole country. The Anglican leaders; men like the Vicar of Birstall, and the local gentry, like Sir John Armytage, having suffered under Cromwell, were not likely to be merciful when it came to carrying out the King's wishes.

One of the entries in the Liversedge Town Book of 1678 says, 'Spent in monthly search for Nonconformists, Quakers and other disaffected persons, 1 shilling.'

This mentions one specific religion; the Quaker Religion which was embraced by none other than the Greene Family. To be specific, it was the second son of John Greene, the founder of the Spen Valley Greenes. This man was named after his father, John.

This was the start of a long association with the Quaker religion and the Spen Valley.

THE QUAKERS

The Society of Friends, the Quakers, was started by George Fox (1629-1691). They got their nickname after Fox told a judge to, *'Tremble at the name of the Lord.'*

Fox travelled the length and breadth of England and on one of his visits to Yorkshire, in 1652, he passed through Hightown and held a meeting at a house there.

Everything was quite peaceful but then someone informed; *'A gentleman of importance,'* who was, *'apparently sharpening a crook to pluck us out of the house and a pike to stab us and was coming with his sword by his side.'*

Someone obviously meant business. Fox and his followers escaped and, *'That night we lay in a wood and it being exceedingly rainy and we were much wet.'*

In fact, Brighouse was the real focal point for Quakerism and it is from the minutes of the Brighouse monthly meetings that we get our records about the Spen Valley. From these we see that the early Quakers were considered highly dangerous by both the civil and the religious authorities. They refused to swear oaths of allegiance to the Crown after 1660 and they refused not only to go to Church, but to pay tithes to the Church. As a result they were persecuted.

They kept detailed Records of Suffering which showed that several Quakers from Oakenshaw, Roberttown, Hightown and Liversedge were thrown into prison and fined. Nine people were arrested in Oakenshaw (which was only a tiny hamlet) and taken as prisoners to York Castle.

The entries from 1660 to 1665 mention a Jonas Lang, blanket-maker of Roberttown and a John Greene from Liversedge.

The Digest of Burials shows a John Greene the Elder who died in 1669.

John Greene the Elder was the second son of the founder of the Liversedge dynasty. We have already met his older brother William who lived in great splendour at Liversedge Hall and who conformed in both politics and religion.

William's brother John was a very different character.

He was born in 1596 and he became a yeoman clothier like most of the Greene family. His house was Upper House in Hightown on the site of the present Upper House Farm, off Hare Park Lane. His home was a substantial building with gardens and an orchard. His farmland bordered Peep Green Common.

John was a staunch supporter of the Puritan side in the Civil War and so was completely opposed to his nephew, who was by now a high ranking Royalist soldier.

But the main reason why he differed from the rest of his family was that he and his wife Bridget were drawn to the Quaker religion. When George Fox came to Hightown to preach they were among the first to become followers.

They formed a Quaker group in Liversedge and as a result were constantly fined and thrown into prison. But perhaps the most cruel punishment was the threat that John and his family would not be allowed to be buried in the churchyard at Hartshead Church.

He overcame this ignominy by preparing his own burial ground in 1665 on the corner of his farmland. This little Sepulchre was also in sight of Hartshead Church and that might well have provided him with some comfort.

He built it in 1665 because that was the first time since the Restoration of the Monarchy in 1660, that he had to deal with a burial. In fact two of the Greene family died in that year.

John's wife Bridget who was 60 years of age and their baby grandson, Solomon. John Greene himself was buried there in 1669.

The Toleration Act was passed in 1689 which ended the denial of burial rights and so this period of persecution came to an end.

There are many such burial grounds dotted about the country, often in isolated places and with little to identify them because proper gravestones were still not officially permitted until 1850.

But this being the Spen Valley, the Greenes were not deterred, so this Sepulchre is very unusual in having lengthy inscriptions on all four of its tombstones.

John's reads as follows, *'Here lyeth the body of John Greene of Liversedge who departed this life the 20th day of the twelfth month anno domini 1669.'*

John Greene's grave, the Sepulcre

His wife Bridget's tombstone is next to it.

Her inscription reads, *'Heare was layed the body of Bridget Greene wife to John Greene of Liversedge the 4th day of the 5th month 1665.'*

Bridget Greene's grave, the Sepulcre

John Greene's son also became a Quaker, John Greene the Younger (born in 1630).

He died in York for his religion and his body was placed in a nameless grave. His wife Elizabeth had borne him eleven children, ten of whom survived. The youngest, Samuel, was born in the year that his father was executed.

He suffered even more than his father as the Record of Suffering shows,

'John Greene of Liversedge in the parish of Burstall and his wife was persecuted in the Bishops Courte for not going to the steeple house and receiving Bread and Wine called sacrament: and after by the Writt de excom: was the said John committed prisoner to Yorke castle the 26th of the 8th month 1675. Released of this imprisonment by death about the 11th of the 5th month 1676.'

John's eldest son Thomas took up the cause of the Quaker religion. By the time that he was a young man, the worst of the persecutions were over, although Thomas was fined for non payment of tithes. He became the leading Quaker of the area. His first wife, Mary is buried in the Sepulchre.

Mary's is the largest of the four tombstones and is raised in the form of an altar.

It bears the touching inscription, *'Here was layed the body of Mary wife of Thomas Greene of Liversedge (aged 18 years, 4 months and 16 days) who departed this life the 3rd day of the 4th month 1684. This was her final testimony, all the world nothing is to me she vice did shvn and vertve did pesve all such shal a reward be given which is their dve that of those ioys they may possess where the wicked cease from troubling and the weary be at rest.'*

Thomas Greene was a wealthy clothier and he lived in a very large house now called Haigh House in Hightown, very probably on the site of the ancient Liversedge Place.

When he bought the house, it was a half timbered building which we now know was built in 1513. He re-built it in stone in the 17th Century style and called it New House. There was a workhouse attached to the house and a beautiful garden full of fruit trees. It's interesting to note that Thomas Greene needed a, *'Deep fosse or ditch which ran round it and was always kept filled with water.'*

So although he was an important man in the township who took a prominent part in managing its affairs, he needed to look after his safety.

The house can still be seen just below The Shears Inn. The back of the house is nearest Halifax Road but you can tell by the glimpses of the front of the house what a magnificent building it once was.

Haigh House, Hightown

After 1756 an eminent Hightown merchant called Haigh bought the house and ever since it has been known as Haigh House. This is where the Quakers held their meetings until 1696 when Jo. Cordingley's farm house was used at Lower Blacup.

But the Quakers began to feel the need for a proper Meeting House and in 1701 Thomas Greene paid for the building of a Friends Meeting House. This was on Townend Lane, now called Quaker Lane.

Attached to it was a burial ground, so now at last the Quakers had their own special burial ground. Thomas's mother Elizabeth was buried here in 1701 and Thomas Greene himself was buried here in 1714.

This meeting house can still be seen on Quaker Lane.

There is one more (tiny) tombstone in the Sepulchre. This dates back to 1665 when John Greene the Elder had to prepare his graveyard. It belongs to Thomas's brother who died aged only two weeks.

His inscription simply reads, '*Here was layd the body of Solomon Greene sonne to John Greene the Younger the 5th of the (?) month 1665.*'

So he lies next to his grandparents and Mary,

When Thomas Greene died, his eldest daughter, Elizabeth (Mary's daughter) inherited his property, including the Sepulchre. This was passed down until 1796 when it was given into the care of the Brighouse Friends.

The lease is for 9,000 years!

This graveyard is a very special place with its clumps of trees and hilltop views. And the words it contains bring history to life. It is testament to a group of people who were prepared to stand up to the authorities and suffer punishment and death rather than give up their ideals.

THE GREENE FAMILY TREE

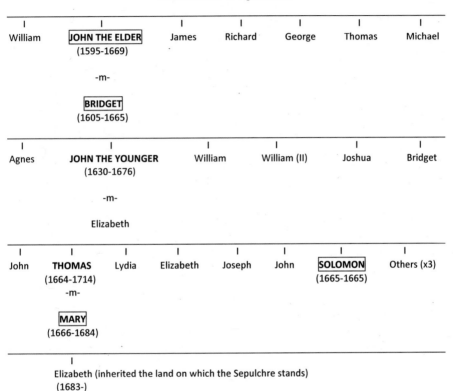

JOHN GREENE -m- Agnes Drake

William	**JOHN THE ELDER** (1595-1669)	James	Richard	George	Thomas	Michael

-m-

BRIDGET (1605-1665)

Agnes	**JOHN THE YOUNGER** (1630-1676)	William	William (II)	Joshua	Bridget

-m-

Elizabeth

John	**THOMAS** (1664-1714)	Lydia	Elizabeth	Joseph	John	**SOLOMON** (1665-1665)	Others (x3)

-m-

MARY (1666-1684)

Elizabeth (inherited the land on which the Sepulchre stands) (1683-)

Key: The four graves in the Sepulchre

Other Nonformist Groups

Although the Quakers suffered the most, all Nonconformists were treated as heretics and hunted down.

Every Justice of the Peace was expected to find them and put them in gaol. No Nonconformist felt safe as they could be informed upon and reported to the authorities.

When James II became King, there were serious worries that the Roman Catholic religion would return and Catholics were hunted down and persecuted. There was relief in 1688 when Willam and Mary became Protestant monarchs.

Religious choice ceased to be such a dangerous affair.

THE END OF THE 17th CENTURY

The Economy

The population, which at the start of the century, was very sparce and had been occupied in farming, was now growing steadily. Most people were involved in some small way in manufacturing and a new dynamic middle class was growing and building fine houses which emulated the aristocracy.

Liversedge was still the most important of the townships. Having been for generations the seat of an important family it attracted a larger population. And the Rayners and Greenes had seen to it that it retained its position of importance. In 1693, an Act was passed *'For granting their Majesties an aid of four shillings in the pound for carrying on a vigorous war with France.'*

The assessments in the Spen Valley show that Liversedge paid over twice as much as Cleckheaton and Heckmondwike and Gomersal.

Transport

Transport was not very well developed and the clothiers depended on carts or horse-back to take their cloth to market.

Ogilby's map of 1675 shows the stage-coach route from York to Chester and the stopping places in our area were; Birstall, Gomersal, Cleckheaton Green (where they stopped at The Nag's Head, now The George) and then via Westgate and Moorbottom up to Hartshead Moor.

This was the main post road and every town had to maintain and repair this road where it passed through their settlement.

The only other highway was the old Roman road through Heckmondwike, Millbridge and Hightown. The remainder of roads were simple tracks or bridleways.

Frank Peel describes these in his book as rough crooked lanes full of treacherous holes filled with liquid mud up to the cart axles.

These were only suitable for pack horses which travelled in long lines with their burdens piled high on their backs. There were very few tracks connecting villages, for example there was nothing to connect Cleckheaton with Liversedge along the Spen Valley.

Local Government

The Spen Valley was governed (as elsewhere) by only a few officials. The main priorities were law enforcement, care of the poorest people in the community and an attempt to keep the highways suitable for road users. That was the sum total of local government.

Law enforcement was carried out by the parish constable from the earliest times until 1856 when the Police Force was introduced. We have already mentioned several of these constables in relation to their grand houses.

It was expected that the parish constable should come from a well respected family and this was always the case.

They were very often wealthy farmers which was a good thing as they were not paid! They were elected annually and it was their duty to prevent disorder in the parish.

The constable had the power of arrest but the only punishment he could carry out was to lock wrong-doers in the stocks for safekeeping until they could be presented to the magistrate. Before doing this he was required to examine all the evidence of a crime and make a report.

The magistrate was usually a person of authority by dint of his wealth and status like the head of the Armytage Family who down the centuries acted as magistrate for Hartshead and Clifton.

Trials and Inquests were often held at local inns such as The Black Horse in Clifton and The Black Bull in Birstall.

The Care of the Poor

As early as 1536, there were regulations ordering collections in the churches for the poor, but the Elizabethan Poor Law of 1601 laid down the foundations for a proper Poor Relief system where local taxes were to be raised to help those who couldn't afford to look after themselves.

This was a very important step in helping the destitute.

Work was to be provided for the unemployed and young people were to be apprenticed. In addition, money was raised for the poor through a Poor Rate which was only paid by the wealthiest people. This rate was set by an official known as an Overseer of the Poor.

Often the Overseers would arrange for paupers to get jobs as domestic servants so that they would live in a household and be cared for.

As was the case with the constables, the overseers were drawn from responsible members of the community. They were usually elected by churchwardens and magistrates.

The work of the constables and overseers was documented in the Towns Books which were annual records kept from the time of Charles II.

There was a third official, again unpaid, and chosen from the middle classes. This was the Surveyor of Highways.

His work involved checking road surfaces and then forcing men from each village to spend four days a year repairing the worst stretches.

He had to present an account of the state of the roads three times a year to the local Justice of the Peace.

CHAPTER 6: THE 18th CENTURY

The Spen Valley was still very rural.

There were only about 1,500 families living there which is just over 6,000 people. This shows how sparse the population was. Most of the open fields had been enclosed into small hedged fields belonging to individual farmers (apart from Cleckheaton).

The land was not so fertile that it would support a growing population by farming alone. This encouraged the dual economy of farming and weaving.

THE DEVELOPMENT OF THE DOMESTIC CLOTH INDUSTRY

Like most areas of the West Riding of Yorkshire, the Spen Valley's wealth was developed from wool.

Daniel Defoe passed this way at the start of the new century and describes a valley filled with manufacturing villages with houses covering the steep hillsides, each having a small enclosure of land, about two to seven acres.

He discovered that the people here were constantly employed in the making of cloth and every house had a Tenter across which they stretched the cloth to bleach in the sun. Everyone had a job; the women and children did the carding and spinning and the men wove the yarn into cloth and dyed the finished product in dye vats.

'I thought it was the most agreeable sight that I ever saw for the hills rising and falling so thick and the valley opening sometimes one way, sometimes another, so that we could see two or three miles away. We could see through the glades almost everyway round us, yet look which way we would, high to the tops and low to the bottoms, it was all the same, innumerable houses and tenters and a white piece upon every tenter. It was a busy landscape.'

Daniel Defoe's book, 'A Tour through the whole island of Great Britain 1724-1727,' provides us with a fascinating survey of the British landscape including our own Spen Valley.

All the processes of woollen manufacture (except fulling) was done by hand in the individual cottages and farmhouses.

This weaver's cottage on the left, with the mullioned windows was built in the 18th Century. The cottage on the right was dated 1666.

Weavers' cottages, Hartshead Lane

The wool was carded first, mainly by the elderly women and small children. This involved breaking up the clumps of fibres in the wool and turning them into individual threads ready for spinning.

The tools used for this process were Cards, square paddles fitted with closely spaced wire pins. A pair of cards brushed the wool between them to straighten out the fibres. These were then dyed in cauldrons over the fire and then spun into yarn, again mainly by women and children in the downstairs room.

A ladder went to the upper floor of the cottage which was often stone flagged to hold the loom, which was worked by men and boys. A row of mullioned windows let in as much light as possible for the weaving process.

The average family would produce up to thirty pieces of cloth a year but most of this would be made in the winter months when farm-work was not as heavy.

There were two other processes which had to be carried on outside the cottages. One was the fulling process. The woven cloth was taken to a fulling mill where it was hammered with heavy fulling stocks driven by a water wheel. This thickened the cloth (this replaced the earlier methods of trampling the cloth which had been soaked in fullers earth and which, as we have seen, gave rise to the surname Walker in medieval times).

The cloth was hung out to dry on Tenter Frames, stretched out to retain its shape (hence the term 'on tenterhooks' referring to the nerves being stretched to breaking point). Tenters were fence-like constructions upon which the lengths of cloth were laid out.

The second process carried on outside the cottages was the finishing process. There were two parts to this. The surface of the cloth had to be brushed up with teasels on a frame called a Nellie and then it was taken to the croppers bench and trimmed with huge iron shears (weighing about 40lbs) to get a smooth surface. This was cloth dressing; the most important and skilled of all the processes. It was carried out by Croppers and the quality of the finished cloth and hence its value depended on them.

These men were highly skilled and well paid. There would be a master cropper and several apprentices aged between 14 and 21 years of age in each cropping shop. They were well rewarded for their strength and skill, earning 20 to 25 shillings a week to the spinners' 5 shillings. Their high level of skills made them into a sort of industrial elite. They were also able to organise themselves into associations as they, unlike the rest of the cloth workers, worked in numbers in workshops and not isolated cottages.

The clothiers collected the finished cloth or Kerseys and took it by ponies or donkeys to cloth markets like the Piece Hall in Halifax. The goods they made were destined for the American colonies but this trade was seriously disrupted by the American War of Independence 1775-1783. Until then, clothiers from the Spen Valley travelled to New York and did business direct with the colonies. They exported carpets, blankets and rough cloth.

The Declaration of Independence crippled this foreign trade. Clothiers had to develop new markets within the British Isles in the growing towns and cities. They also started to trade with Europe.

In the 18th Century some yeomen clothiers practised cloth manufacturing and marketing on a larger scale. They operated by 'putting out' the work to local people and collecting the woven cloth but they had their own workshops where they 'finished' the cloth and then they took it to the Cloth Halls in Leeds and Halifax.

These clothiers did their own marketing and selling. Jeremy Lane in Heckmondwike is called after Jeremy Firth (1750-1822), a merchant who travelled to London to sell his cloth (his house was on Jeremy Lane).

John Taylor of Gomersal also travelled to London where he gained a valuable contract for army uniforms.

If Daniel Defoe had visited the area towards the end of the century he would have seen changes. New machinery was being invented. The Flying Shuttle loom was not only faster but could be operated by one man.

The Spinning Jenny enabled yarn to be produced at a faster rate to keep up with the hungry looms. The Carding Machine was invented in 1775 and this helped speed up the preparation of wool for spinning (the first one locally was at Strawberry Bank Watermill in Liversedge).

The woollen industry did not become fully mechanised until the second half of the 19th Century but some master clothiers began to see the future. Instead of 'putting out' the individual tasks to the self employed cottage-based spinner or weaver, they could bring all the processes together under one roof. They could become mill owners.

At first croppers did well because the clothiers and the new millowners sent their cloth to the Dressing Shop for finishing and their workload was much increased. Unfortunately for them, in 1787 a machine was invented in Sheffield which mechanised their work.

This consisted of two pairs of mounted shears which passed over the cloth to remove the Nap. One man could now do the work of ten skilled croppers. Enoch and James Taylor, iron founders in Marsden, got the patent to produce Shearing Machines locally.

Another new machine had actually been invented back in 1551 but had been banned from use by the government to protect the employment prospects of those in the finishing trade. This was the Gig Mill.

This could raise the hairy surface of the cloth (the nap) mechanically, prior to it being trimmed. It was a very simple device which consisted of a revolving drum into which twelve rows of teasels were set. The cloth was passed over these with the aid of rollers.

There were a few gig mills in the Huddersfield area but it was not until 1805 that William Horsfall introduced shearing machinery in his mill in Marsden (the town where they were made) and 1809 when these new-fangled machines arrived in the Spen Valley, at a mill rented by William Cartwright; Rawfolds mill in Liversedge.

GOMERSAL

Gomersal had a number of successful clothiers and some of these began to trade as merchants They built large workshops near their homes and although the processes involved in making their cloth were still the traditional hand processes, these were the prototype of Factory Buildings.

John Taylor's large workshop was situated at the side of his home. Thomas Burnley's was very possibly part of the building at Grove Square, also in Oxford Road.

The Porritts were another prosperous family. Jonathan Porritt (born in 1713) continued down the traditional route of acting as a master clothier. He employed local weavers in the Gomersal and Birstall area to work for him and he was so successful, that by the late 1750's he kept some thirty donkeys in Gomersal to regularly take kerseys to sell at Leeds Cloth Hall. There he had seven stands to sell his goods.

Not surprisingly he became tired of travelling to and fro from Leeds and so he collaborated with John Taylor and Thomas Burnley to build their own Cloth Hall near the top of Spen Lane (this only operated until 1793 because of opposition from Leeds merchants).

The second half of the century saw the real start of the Industrial Revolution with the advent of water-powered machinery.

John Taylor, who had inherited Red House, transferred his workshop at his home, to Hunsworth in the valley of the Spen river, where there was the running water needed for dying and scouring and most importantly for turning the new machinery. There was still a workshop near the house which was used for some finishing processes.

This mill made army cloths known as Common Thick-un's which were needed to clothe the army fighting in North America and later in the century in the wars with France, from 1793 to 1815.

This was boom time for the army cloth trade and John Tayler prospered. He turned Red House, into a more fashionable residence with a new frontage and elegant hallway. The old farmhouse nearby was demolished and pleasant gardens laid out. A barn and a cart shed were built at the top of the garden for easy access to the family's main fields in the Cliffe Lane area. These buildings can still be seen today.

The Taylor Family epitomises the changes made over the previous two hundred years. In the 16th Century. Thomas Taylor was rich enough to buy land and build a farmhouse; his grandson William built the very fine Red House in the 17th Century and his grandson John was enterprising enough to build a water-driven mill in the Spen Valley at Hunsworth and to follow the fashions of his time in improving his home. The Taylors now began participating in public affairs. These were prosperous times. John Taylor also built a chapel, near his home. And this, as we will later see, reflects another change.

Garden Gate, Red House

Red House, Gomersal

The Barn at Red House

William Burnley's son Thomas also prospered. In 1752, he moved into Pollard Hall as a tenant. There he started the processes of dyeing and finishing cloth. He then moved from his workshop at Pollard Hall, to a factory which had been built nearby on the site of the short-lived Cloth Hall.

Little Gomersal

In the 18th Century, Little Gomersal still consisted of a handful of cottages grouped around the village green, with two or three larger houses on the outskirts. The Domestic Industry was carried out in these cottages.

Spen

The Spen hamlet passed to the Smythe family and this ended the Manorial System here.

The Spen corn mill was re-built to accommodate more machinery and this meant more extensive channeling of the water course to ensure a good head of water to the mill.

A new mill house was built and one of the first families who lived here was the Mann Family. The mill dam is still known locally as Harry Mann Dam after the last of the Mann family to work at the mill.

Heckmondwike

The clothiers of Heckmondwike specialised in Heavy Woollens and towards the end of the century, the village became the centre of a thriving blanket weaving industry. These blankets were woven on hand looms usually in the upstairs rooms of the cottages.

Merchants came to Heckmondwike on Mondays and Thursdays to buy the finished blankets. During the 18th Century, this trade was carried out at The George Inn on Westgate.

By 1811 the trade had expanded so much that the landlord of the Inn, Francis Popplewell, decided special premises should be built for the blanket weavers of Heckmondwike to sell their cloth, so the first Blanket Hall was built on land behind the inn.

A new and larger blanket hall was needed by 1839, but unfortunately, it was about this time that control of the blanket trade shifted to the large millowner and the blanket hall fell into disuse.

But Blanket Hall Street still survives today.

Although Heckmondwike was still only a village, a regular market was held on the streets nearby the Green from 1760 when the main stalls sold meat, fish and clogs. It was held on Saturdays. It didn't receive its official charter until 1810.

Heckmondwike grew considerably in the 18th Century and began to overtake its older neighbour, Liversedge, in terms of industrial activity.

CLECKHEATON

We have already seen that Cleckheaton came late to industrial development because of the strong degree of manorial control by the Richardson Family, who were not a commercial family.

Cleckheaton people remained farmers until 1795 when the open fields were finally enclosed.

The preamble to the Enclosure Act, signed by Mr. Henry Brooke says,

'There are within the township of Cleckheaton in the Parish of Birstall, certain open fields commonly known by the names of the Lower Whitecliffe, Upper Whitecliffe, Peaselands, Townsteads, Chearbarrows and the Tofts, containing 180 acres and three Open Stinted Pastures called Hunsworth Moor and two Greens containing together about 30 acres.'

All of these were divided up between the major landowners of the village in an Act of Enclosure, which described itself as, *'An Act for dividing, allocating and enclosing the open fields, several commons, moors and waste grounds within the hamlets of Cleckheaton and Scholes.'*

This also included the village greens: Upper Green where the park is now situated and Lower Green which is the old market square, on Market Street in Cleckheaton.

The Cleckheaton Enclosure Map is dated February 14th 1797, In the 35th Year of the reign of King George III.

A map of 1802, surveyed by Alexander Calvert Richmond shows the names of the open fields and how they have now been divided up into separate Lots and the names of the new owners are carefully written in. Richard Beaumont Esq. and Diana his wife got the lion's share and Mr. John Brooke also gained a lot of land.

Other names that are dotted about the former open fields and greens are Mr. George Armitage, Jonas Yates, Obadiah Brooke, Thomas Horncastle, Sam Taylor and Hannah Kitson. Hunsworth Moor was divided between these landowners but two more names appear here; Mr. Richard Booth and the Hon. Lumley Savile.

Some of the names of the open fields and indeed the landowners who bought them up are still in evidence today, in street names and buildings.

But this late date for enclosing the open fields may be the reason that card setting was the only important activity because it could be readily combined with the practice of open field farming and most of it was carried out by women and children in the home.

Their cottages were built along little lanes and courts, or Yards, between Tofts Lane and Hunsworth Moor Road as they had been since the Middle Ages.

The beck flowing from near Blacup Farm and known as Blacup Beck formed the boundary with Liversedge. This beck provided water power for the water wheel at Old Robin Mill which can still be seen behind the Post Office.

It is the oldest surviving mill in Cleckheaton, being a late 18th Century Fulling and Scribbling mill, showing that there was some cloth manufacture starting to develop. Blacup Beck is now culverted but it runs parallel with the 1740 Leeds to Elland Turnpike Road which we now know as Westgate.

There were no more through roads in Cleckheaton. There was no proper road along the valley towards Littletown until a Turnpike Road was built in 1806. Once the enclosures happened, there was great resentment and hardship as the people of Cleckheaton lost their livelihoods just at the time when a trade depression (caused by the Napoleonic War) had hit the region.

LIVERSEDGE

Liversedge ceased to be the most important of the Spen Valley towns in the 18th Century mainly because of the fact that there were no longer great entrepreneurs to lead the way in industrial development.

There were small family concerns like Obadiah Lang and Sons who were blanket makers in Littletown, but nothing on the scale of Heckmondwike's developing industry.

The Greene family gradually disappeared from the scene, exhausting the wealth of their predecessors. In 1746, Samuel Greene was the last of the family to sign the Town's Books in an official capacity.

The old halls which they had owned passed to new families. The age of the Liversedge dynasties was over. History had repeated itself.

OTHER INDUSTRIES

Other industrial activity was linked to the manufacture of cloth in the Spen Valley.

Card Setting

The production of hand cards, for carding wool, was introduced by the Overend family of Scholes at the end of the 17th Century.

Wire was cut into suitable lengths by hand shears and the staples were inserted into the leather foundation which was then nailed on to wooden paddles. This was known as Card Setting, a job mainly done by women and children who earned starvation wages from this very tedious job.

Many children became crippled and deformed after sitting hunched over their work, sitting on low stools or on the cottage doorstep. Their eyesight suffered too. The centres for this industry were Cleckheaton and Scholes.

Machinery was not introduced on a large scale until the start of the 19th Century although carding machines were being used in mills in Cleckheaton and Scholes from the 1780's by the Overends and also the Quaker family most associated with the trade, the Croslands of Oldfieldnook. In these machines the wire was fixed into a cylinder.

Wire Drawing

This was the twin industry of card making. It was often dangerous work because of the processes involved.

The iron wires were drawn through holes of various sizes to get the correct diameter and then they were heated in a furnace. Next they were cleaned in oil of vitriol which was highly corrosive to the skin. The other danger was that if the wires snapped during the drawing process it could lead to serious injuries.

This industry developed in Cleckheaton because of the importance of the carding industry but it did become commonplace throughout the Spen Valley.

Tanning

This was once one of the most common industries throughout Britain; carried out on a small scale and usually specialising in one particular leather product.

There were Tanneries at Hartshead and Spen Lane, Gomersal. The workers' cottages and the manager's house still stand at Hartshead and much of the tannery building still exists in Gomersal. And on Valley Road, not far from Providence Place Chapel stood Edward Brook's tannery, founded in 1720. There was also a tannery at the top of Clough Lane, Liversedge.

The processes involved were the strengthening of the animal skin to make it resistant to decay. This made use of either vegetable tannages made out of oak bark or mineral tannages which were a mix of alum, flour, salt and oil.

The tannery site consisted of a series of pits. One for soaking to wash and soften the hide, lime pits to remove hair, one where the lime was neutralised and the skin plumped up, and tan pits where the leather was soaked in the tanning liquor.

Currying

This was a similar process to the cropping industry in the manufacture of textiles in that it was the highly specialised part of the production of leather; the art of dressing the leather for whatever the finished product might be; shoes or saddlery or card setting. The leather for shoes and boots would be sent to a shoemaker, or Cordwainer and for saddles and harnesses to a Saddler.

All these family trades were passed on through the generations. This particular craft involved the stretching and finishing of the tanned leather.

The stretching of the leather was done on frames and scrubbed to soften it to remove any remaining tanning fluid. This was hard physical work. The really skilful stage was the dressing of the skins to make them smooth, flexible and strong. The hides were then cut to size and the actual currying took place, massaging cod liver oil and tallow into the leather.

The Organisation of Trades

Most villages in the Spen Valley had trades like the curriers.

Each trade had a Master and Apprentices, many of whom lived in the household of the master's family. Apprenticeships could be as long as seven years from the age of fourteen. During that time the apprentice was not paid a wage but was fed and clothed by his master. When he was twenty-one, he would be allowed to leave and carry out the trade on his own.

After 1814, the seven year apprenticeship scheme was ended by law and this caused a great deal of uncertainty, especially at a time of growing mechanisation in industry.

TRANSPORT

For most of the century, industry and commerce was on a very limited scale. The Domestic System hardly progressed from previous centuries.

One of the main problems facing manufacturers was the difficulty of transporting their goods. The roads were very poor.

Where there is now the A649 Halifax road (the old Roman road) there was a paved packhorse route called the High Street, along which had grown a number of inns where travellers and their packhorses could rest.

The Shears Inn for example, was built in 1753 for this purpose. And The Packhorse Inn built at an important crossroads on Hartshead Moor.

As early as the 17th Century, increased traffic, caused by the growth of the woollen industry, was putting pressure on such packhorse routes. In fact in 1663 it was decided by a Turnpike Act that road users should pay for the maintenance of roads.

But it was not until the 18th Century that the Spen Valley got any Turnpike Roads. Halifax Road was improved to form one of the earliest turnpike roads in 1740. This was the Wakefield to Halifax turnpike road.

Turnpike roads were built by Turnpike Trusts; groups of businessmen who invested their money in road building and who then re-couped their money by charging tolls for road users, who were stopped at the Toll Bars. This was a great improvement on the practice of local villagers repairing the worst stretches of dirt roads.

Other turnpike roads followed. One, dating from 1740, followed the old packhorse route from Birstall up to Gomersal, down Spen Bank, through Cleckheaton and along Westgate, then on to Moorside and High Moor Lane and over Hartshead Moor. This was the Leeds to Elland Turnpike.

Another one, built in 1765, went from Birstall to Millbridge, up Roberttown Lane, to Roberttown, down Far Common Road (past Peep Green Common) and then past Mirfield Moor and on to Huddersfield. This was a new routeway. It was called the Birstall and Huddersfield Turnpike Trust.

The practice of charging local people for the use of the roads which had always been free caused some bitterness and in 1753, the toll bars at Millbridge and Bailiff Bridge were attacked by rioters!

In 1766 a law was passed which stated that all Turnpikes had to set up milestones as a guide to travellers.

So a start was made to improve communications and once the new roads were built there was an impetus to trade. Mail coaches too were able to travel more easily. In 1784, Palmer's mail coaches started up in business.

Wayside inns grew up to accommodate travellers and provide refreshment for them and their horses. These inns were often used for public meetings and courts, for example The Black Bull at Birstall held magistrates' sessions.

It's still possible to see the original panelling, the magistrate's box and the prisoner's dock in the upstairs room here.

The Black Bull, Birstall

Most of these wayside inns brewed their own beer. The White Horse Inn at Gomersal Hill Top and The Nags Head (now The George) in Cleckheaton, are typical examples. They were both sited at crossroads on long-distance routes.

Some roads were the result of another kind of Act of Parliament. The 1795 Enclosure Act for Cleckheaton, altered the fields and pastures of the town and necessitated the building of roads across former open fields. Many of these roads took the name of the former field on which it was built, for example Whitcliffe Road on the former White Cliffe Field.

The Act stipulated the need for an Overseer of Roads to ensure that they were kept in good order by the several land-owners. It also stated that the surveyor would be appointed, *'By the townspeople at the Feast of St Michaelmas and receive a salary for his or her trouble.'*

It even set out where footpaths should go, and where a stone quarry and gravel pits should be set up for repairing the roads.

Some roads declined in importance. For example Moor Lane in Gomersal was once a very wide Drove Road down which cattle were driven on to the commons. It was also a well populated part of the village.

And the bridle path that now crosses Popeley Fields and down Garfit Hill to the church at Birstall was once an important roadway. It is the road which Charlotte Bronte describes in 'Jane Eyre' when her heroine walks from Birstall to Liversedge.

But packhorses remained the main method of transport throughout the century. Kilpin Hill in Heckmondwike got its name from a famous keeper of packhorses and stage wagons who lived in a white house at the top of the hill and who controlled the transport business of the day.

So, wheeled vehicles were not common in the 18th Century and the bad state of the roads, which in most cases were still bridleways, remained a real handicap to traders.

There was no alternative transport in the Spen Valley because of the lack of navigable rivers or man-made canals. It was only towards the end of the century that change speeded up and with it, the traffic.

NONCONFORMITY IN THE 18th CENTURY

The Spen Valley remained a hotbed of Nonconformity.

From the reign of Charles II, dissenters met in isolated farmhouses, for example Egypt Farm in Cleckheaton. There were several different types of Nonconformity; Presbyterians, Congregationalists, Quakers and so on. Then from the 1740's, Methodism began to spread.

John Wesley and the Methodists

Wesley's life spanned the 18th Century (1703-1791). The son of a clergyman, he was ordained into the Anglican Church and indeed, he never really left it. John Wesley first preached in Birstall on 26th May 1742. By the following year there were meeting places in Cleckheaton, Birstall, Gomersal and Liversedge where it was recorded that, *'Mr. John Wesley and Mr. Charles Wesley and several other strangers teach.'*

Wesley frequently preached to vast crowds in the open air but gradually purpose built chapels were erected, the first at Birstall in 1750. A second chapel with a thatched roof was opened in Hightown in 1774 and for the rest of the century these two buildings were the only methodist premises. Most methodists worshipped in private houses and later when the numbers soared, in farm barns.

Wesley preached at the opening of the Theyked Chapel (thatched chapel) at Hightown Heights in April 1774 (this is now a building containing two cottages opposite Hightown Post Office).

He was a friend of The Taylors of Red House and often stayed with them when he was in the district. Another of his hosts was Joe Cordingley of Lower Blacup Farm. Upper and Lower Blacup farms had been meeting places for the Quaker religion and now they became centres of Methodism. John Nelson, from Birstall was converted by John Wesley and he became one of his most important preachers.

Lower Blacup Farm, Cleckheaton

The Quakers

This religion continued to flourish because, after the death of Thomas Greene in 1714, the leading role in the story of the Quakers was taken up by the Crosland family.

In 1697, Robert and Martha Crosland moved from Upper Blacup to Scholes.

They built a house called Oldfieldnook and began a card-making business from there. This had now become a very profitable occupation within the woollen industry and in 1739, their son Robert built the oldest part of the present day house, which is an impressive building with magnificent gardens. He was a well respected man; he was an Overseer of the Poor and he helped consolidate the Quaker movement in the village of Scholes.

The Moravians

They were a Protestant Sect from Moravia, now part of the Czech Republic. At first when they settled in this country, they were closely connected with the early Methodists.

By 1740, they had fallen out with John Wesley's church because of his close connection with the Anglican church. They settled in many parts of Yorkshire and wherever they went, they built schools. The Moravian Brethren came to Little Gomersal in 1751 when they built a community between Upper and Lower Lane. They built their first church and two schools, one at either end of the church.

The Moravian Church, Little Gomersal

The Moravian community became quite large with two and three storey cottages built at the end of the 18th Century and early 19th Century. One of their buildings was known as the Sisters' House, a brick built house on Lower Lane, possibly the home of Moravian Sisters.

NONCONFORMISM AND POLITICS

Nonconformists were usually radical in their politics and a good example of this is Dr. Joseph Priestley (1733-1804).

He was born on a farm at Field Head not far from Oakwell Hall but when he was only six years old, his mother died and he went to live with his aunt and uncle, the Keighleys, in Heckmondwike. They lived in the Old Hall in Heckmondwike.

Old Hall, Heckmondwike

Priestley was brought up as a strict Puritan. He became a philosopher but it was his work in chemistry and in particular his discovery of oxygen, which was to make him famous. As with many Puritans, he was radical in his politics and he was a great supporter of the French Revolution and the struggle of the French people to throw off the rule of monarchy and aristocracy. This made him very unpopular in the country as a whole and he had to flee to America where his ideas were accepted more readily.

MORE EIGHTEENTH CENTURY BUILDINGS

The Dumb Steeple

This monument was built in the early part of the century but probably replaced an even earlier monument.

The Steeple part of the name suggests a religious connection and the proximity to Kirklees Priory gives that credence. The Dumb could come from the Latin 'Domini,' meaning Lord's Steeple.

It could also mean 'doomed' referring to the closing down of the Priory by Henry VIII.

Whitechapel

The Church of England continued to remain less popular with Spen people. The Chapel of Ease had been used by the Puritans between 1649 and 1660. After the Restoration of the Monarchy in 1660, there were not enough Anglicans to fill the church and it fell into disrepair. It is recorded that, *'Sheep grazed in the churchyard and their lambs sheltered in the ruins.'*

In 1706, the church was re-built and it was from this time that it took its name Ye Olde Whitechapel in the North because it was whitewashed outside. A stone above the door shows the date when it was re-built. It was becoming better attended because the vicars there were affiliating themselves to the methodist cause. It was from this time that Whitechapel was granted the right of burial and there are still gravestones in the churchyard from this time.

John Wesley himself preached at Whitechapel in 1788. It was the old adage, *'If you can't beat them join them!'*

By 1820, the church was not big enough and had to be re-built yet again.

White Lee Jail

At the end of the 18th Century, a jail for debtors had been built on Jail Road at White Lee.

We hear something about this because the famous prison reformer, John Howard visited it and described it as, *'Having two work rooms and a dark room for the unruly.'*

He liked the fact that the male and female debtors were housed separately. In 1791, on his second visit, he found the prison to be very dirty and the last keeper of the prison had, *'Died by drink.'*

Drink was also being bought in the prison, by those prisoners who could afford it. John Wesley preached there so it is hoped that his sermons provided the moral uplift that was needed!

By the end of the century, the prison closed and Wakefield became the town which accommodated the sinners of Spen. Jail Road however remains.

Other reminders of this time include a variety of buildings.

Roe Head School was built at the turn of the century. This was the school which the young Charlotte Bronte and her sisters attended. It was built on the former main Leeds to Huddersfield road, now Far Common Road in Roberttown.

Kirklees Hall was re-modelled and turned into a very fashionable residence by the Armytage Family.

In 1764, Joseph Bilton, a business man from Leeds, built Healds House, a large and stately manor as befit a wealthy man and Overseer of the Poor. It was one of the most fashionable residences, as well as being one of the largest, in the Spen Valley.

Healds House incorporates an original house built by Richard Rayner. It was bought, in 1795, by the Reverend Hammond Roberson and much more of him later.

In 1740 there was a Workhouse in Roberttown and in one of the Towns Books we see a member of the old noble de Liversedge family residing there!

In 1762, the Overseers of Gomersal decided to build a workhouse in Muffit Lane, because they wanted to deter people from claiming poor relief. Every parish was responsible for its own poor. Money was raised through a poor rate which was a tax levied on the wealthy. So the more poor people there were in a parish, the higher the poor rate.

Those paying for this were becoming more and more resentful and the building of workhouses seemed a better alternative, especially if they were made into in-hospitable places.

More workhouses were built, at Heckmondwike, Liversedge and White Lee. At first they were occupied by the very needy; vagrants, those who were unable to care for themselves and the physically handicapped.

But by the end of the century these workhouses were full to capacity. There obviously was plenty of poverty in the valley.

In 1724 and 1725, wars on the Continent caused economic depression.

In 1745, the Jacobite Rebellion saw more soldiers passing through and men being Pressed into service, for the Yorkshire Buffs, a regiment hastily put together to help stop a Scottish advance south to London.

The American War of Independence hit trade with North America hard and finally the French Revolutionary Wars at the end of the century caused yet more hardship.

Great Gomersal:

From the Township Map of 1839:

Showing How The Settlement Developed:

Key to Map:

1. **Bradford – Dewsbury Turnpike Road**
2. **Peel House**
3. **Moor Lane**
4. **Grove Square**
5. **Grove Chapel**
6. **Glebe (Church) Lands**
7. **Church Wood**
8. **Gomersal Mills**
9. **Pollard Hall**
10. **Red House**
11. **Methodist Chapel**
12. **Gomersal Hall**
13. **Holme – Lane End and Heckmondwike Turnpike Road**

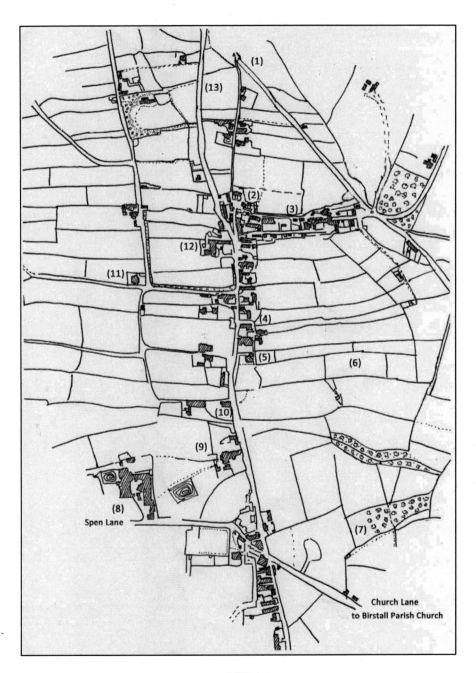

Cleckheaton:

From the Township Map of 1802:

Following the Act of Enclosures:

Key to Map:

1. **Hunsworth Moor Road**
2. **Upper Green**
3. **Lower Green**
4. **Old Robin Mill**
5. **Leeds – Elland Turnpike Road**
6. **Tofts Lane**

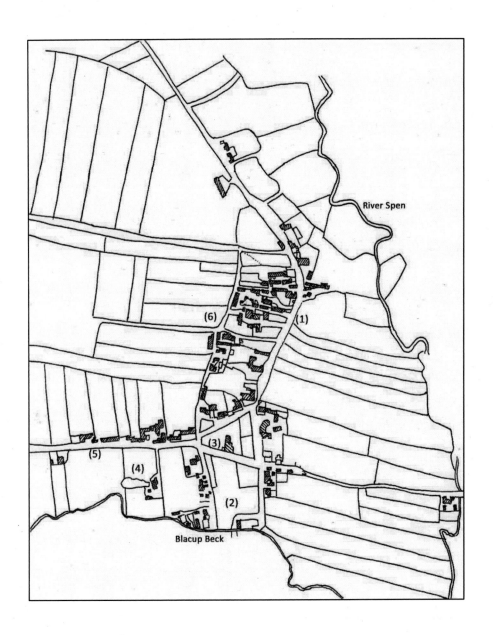

River Spen

(6)

(1)

(3)

(5)

(4)

(2)

Blacup Beck

Liversedge:

From the Township Map of 1804:

Key to Map:

1. Rawfolds Mill
2. Primrose Lane
3. River Spen
4. Clough House
5. Quaker House
6. Quaker Lane
7. Middle Hall
8. Lower Hall
9. Knowler Hill
10. Haigh House
11. Shears Inn
12. Lands Beck
13. Clough Beck
14. Bullace Trees Farm

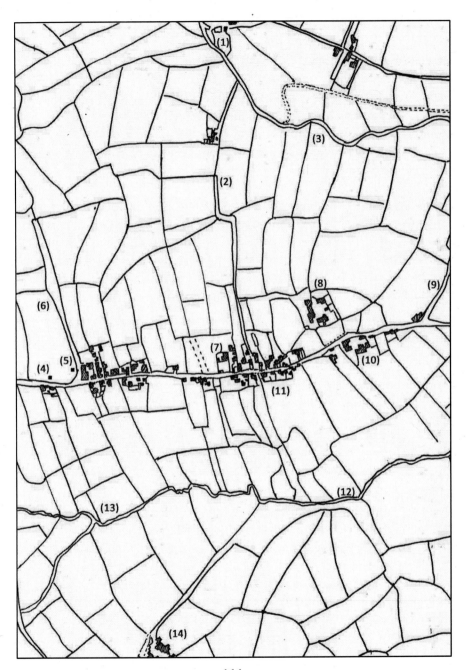

CHAPTER 7: THE 19th CENTURY

POVERTY AND POLITICAL AND SOCIAL UNREST

Early in the 1800's, there was a reference in the Towns Books to a subscription among the 'well to do' in the Spen Valley which was intended to help their poor neighbours. Local committees were formed and food and clothing was doled out; flannel clothing and clogs and bacon, salt beef, and oatcakes.

There were many reasons why the wealthier people had to step in with emergency rations. One was the war now being fought against the French.

The Napoleonic War had crippled commerce and work was scarce. Exports and food imports were virtually nil and this meant that food prices were going up at a time when people could not earn more money.

There were also changes in manufacturing with the introduction of machinery. This was starting to cause even more unemployment.

The situation was getting out of hand.

Starving people began banding together at two gathering places`; Dewsbury Moor and Hartshead Moor. The constables had their hands full.

There was no Police Force until 1856 and policing was still done by the unpaid parish constable. He could arrest wrongdoers and lock them in the stocks for safekeeping before handing them over to the magistrate. There was absolutely no way of controlling such large numbers of hungry, unemployed men and women.

By a strange twist; the handing out of charity by the well to do, resulted in changes in local government in the Liversedge area because the three parts of the town; Hightown, Littletown and Roberttown all quarrelled as each felt they were not getting enough of the provisions!

The Reverend Hammond Roberson, who had come to live in Healds Hall in 1795, when he became curate of Hartshead Church, decided to settle the matter. He called a town's meeting in 1804, over which he presided.

At this meeting it was decided that the constable and the overseer of the poor (often wealthy men) would no longer be able to look after public business as they had done since medieval times. In future, a committee of twelve men should be sworn into office to conduct public affairs. This marks the beginning of a local government model which was then adopted in Heckmondwike and Cleckheaton. It also eroded the powers of the richer families even further.

But despite these positive changes, the country as a whole was experiencing turbulent times. The Spen Valley was no different to elsewhere in this.

THE CAUSES OF POVERTY

The main problem was the high cost of living. This was caused by the disastrous harvests in the years between 1809 and 1812. The price of wheat reached its highest in the spring of 1812. There were food riots throughout the North of England.

The economic crisis caused by war only made things worse.

In 1812, Britain had been fighting the French in the longest period of warfare for a century. The war had started in 1793 and by 1807, the Emperor, Napoleon Bonaparte ruled most of Europe. But after the destruction of his fleet in 1805 at the Battle of Trafalgar, he abandoned his planned invasion of Britain and switched to an economic war.

He blockaded British ships and cut off British trade with much of Europe and North and South America. Britain retaliated in 1807 with the Orders in Council whereby the British navy could board and inspect ships sailing to France.

This badly damaged Britain's economy as trade with America fell when President Thomas Jefferson, fed up with French and British interference with American shipping, put an embargo on all foreign trade.

Food, particularly wheat, could no longer be imported. The working classes suffered the most. Their staple diet was now oatcakes not bread. British exports were very badly affected; piles of cloth were stagnating in the cloth halls. Some employers started using any labour saving devices that were available to cut labour costs and so many workers became unemployed. Cloth workers, among other trades people were reaching the point of destitution.

Shortages of food, unemployment, poverty, high prices, low wages and stagnating trade. This was common in most areas of Britain and especially in the areas which were developing industry on a larger scale; the areas where there was a growing concentration of working classes. Working class protests flared up in 1811 in Nottinghamshire where workmen were in open revolt. This was because their situation was being made even more serious by the introduction of machinery in the hosiery and lace factories.

THE LUDDITES

The political climate was ripe for rebellion. Because of the French Revolution, radicalism had gained strength, and the authorities, terrified of this new atmosphere, closed off all legitimate channels of protest and political activity. So trade unions and strikes were banned by the Combination Act of 1799, as were protest meetings.

Machine breaking was the obvious tactic for those thrown out of work by the new machinery. It stopped work as effectively as a strike. But if done secretly, it protected those involved. And this is what happened in Nottinghamshire in 1811 when workers in the hosiery and lace industries organised themselves into bands under the leadership of someone calling himself Ned Ludd, a man whose identity was never discovered.

It was a highly organised movement requiring a strict oath of secrecy and dedicated to the smashing of the hated machinery. The taking of the secret oath was known as Twisting In to represent the many twisted yarns making up a strong yarn.

The Government, alarmed by the Luddites' lawlessness, made it a capital offence to destroy machinery, but the movement grew and spread from the stocking makers of Nottinghamshire to Lancashire and Cheshire where it spread amongst the weavers and then to Yorkshire where it found a breeding ground among the textile workers in the finishing trade.

The Government now began billeting troops in all the areas where trouble was brewing. The local constables could not have coped with trouble on such a scale!

So how was law and order controlled in 1812?

The Home Secretary was head of a very small Home Office and he and his two under secretaries took a hard line against any form of insurrection. This is why machine breaking was made a capital offence in February, as was oath taking in May. The feeling was that there was an imminent threat that the working classes were planning an uprising similar to the one in France, which in turn had been influenced by the American revolutionaries. Home Office orders were carried out by the Lord Lieutenants in the counties. They could raise volunteer forces. They controlled the main group of lawkeepers, the local magistrates who were usually landowners.

Their powers were to read the Riot Act to a disorderly crowd to ensure it dispersed, and to enrol special constables to help the parish constable in times of trouble. If that didn't work they could bring in local volunteer forces or even request the Home Office to send in the army. The special constables were enrolled from the wealthier members of the community. They were conscripted by the Watch and Ward Act and they carried out arms searches and patrols and enforced curfews.

THE YORKSHIRE LUDDITES

In Yorkshire, the textile workers most badly affected by the new machines were the croppers. The hand croppers were angered by the introduction of the new shearing frames and gig mills which were shutting down the workshops on which their trade had been centred.

Traditionally, the nap on cloth had been raised by hand but gig mills did this mechanically. In 1809, the protective legislation banning machinery was lifted and hard pressed clothiers introduced gig mills to cut down on costs. There followed a wave of attacks on these hated mills and soon many gig mills had been stopped by the croppers.

They were similarly opposed to shearing machinery. They totally rejected mechanical cropping because each water-driven shearing frame did the work of ten men.

Croppers were highly skilled workers, manipulating the huge shears which smoothed the surface of the woollen cloth. They were well paid because the quality and hence the value of the finished cloth depended on them. Their livelihood was now jeopardised.

The local manufacturers of the new shearing machines were Enoch and James Taylor who had a large iron foundry in Marsden and who made, among other things, agricultural equipment and tools such as hammers. Ironically it was these very sledge-hammers which the Luddites used in their campaign of machine breaking. They nick- named them Enochs and stated that, *'Enoch hath made them, Enoch shall break them!'*

The old and new systems of shearing were represented in the Spen Valley by two men. John Jackson, a cloth dresser, owned quite a large workshop at the top of Quilley Lane (now Hare Park Lane). William Cartwright rented a water-powered mill on the River Spen at Liversedge; Rawfolds Mill, which had been fitted with new machinery since 1809.

Cartwright was immortalised in Charlotte Bronte's novel 'Shirley,' a story which describes the Luddites' struggle.

She depicts him as being shrewd and far-sighted and; *'Keen o' making brass and getting forwards.'*

Jackson's workshop had been really profitable before this new competition from Cartwright. The men there had earned good wages, but now the cropping shop lost profits and men had to be laid off.

One of the men who lost his job, was William Hall of Parkin Hoyle on Hartshead Lane. He had learnt his trade at Jackson's but the foreman, William Fearnside, assured him that he would be taken on again if trade improved. Hall managed to get a job at Wood's workshop at Longroyd Bridge in Huddersfield and spent his weekends visiting his family in Liversedge.

Huddersfield was the epicentre of Luddism in Yorkshire. It's very likely that the movement began here as early as 1801. The Luddite headquarters were at John Wood's workshop at Longroyd Bridge. George Mellor, Wood's stepson, virtually ran the business and it's believed that he was the chief 'Ludd' of the area.

Other key Luddites were Thomas Smith, John and Benjamin Walker and Thomas Booth. Mellor's right hand man, William Thorpe, worked at Fisher's cropping shop nearby.

It was easy enough to organise themselves effectively, given that there were several men working legitimately together, unlike the isolated domestic workers. The Huddersfield Cloth Dressers Society had set up an Institution to try to get round the banning of Trades Unions and this had petitioned the Government about their grievances.

But by 1806 even this was regarded as seditious and had been dismantled; the workers had no legal outlets left.

So it was at Wood's workshop that William Hall found employment and much more. He swore his oath to the Luddite cause and brought its ideas back to Liversedge. There he met with his former workmates at The Shears Inn and let them in on the exciting meetings he was attending in Huddersfield.

The Shears was the most substantial building in the locality, according to Frank Peel. Most of the surrounding properties were ordinary cottages. Peel believed it was the most popular inn for the croppers and that they were good customers for the landlord's ale when they had money in their pockets.

The disgruntled croppers assembled to listen to what was happening in Huddersfield and eventually it was arranged that Hall should invite John Walker and Thomas Booth to meet them.

The Shears Inn, Hightown, Liversedge

This meeting, in February 1812, held in the upper room at The Shears, was attended by croppers from Cleckheaton, Gomersal, Birstall, Mirfield, Brighouse and Elland. In his book on the 'Risings of the Luddites,' Frank Peel describes this meeting in great detail; how Walker, the jolly one of the speakers sang to them the Croppers' Song and how the fiery orator Thomas Brook inspired his listeners to action.

He describes an old oak-cased clock in the corner of the room with a clear sounding bell and the long tables down the room at which the drinkers sat and he talks about a solemn oath of secrecy being administered to all present. Their names were then taken down by the vigilant watchmen who had kept careful guard at the door and at the bottom of the steps.

The first thing they planned to do was to stop a delivery of shearing machines bound for Cartwright's mill. This was a new tactic. Destroy the machines before they even arrived at the mill.

Peel thought that had James Lister, the landlord, been aware of the real object of the meeting he would certainly have placed his veto upon it for although he naturally agreed with the men who had been such excellent customers, he prided himself as being above all things a law-abiding citizen.

MACHINE BREAKING

As nothing was known about the formation of the Spen Valley Luddites, the machines were sent without armed guards and on the usual route from Marsden.

So the band of masked men, laying in wait on Hartshead Moor, had the advantage. Everything went well for them because the snowy weather meant that the two wagons were delayed. The waggoners had thought that they could make the journey in daylight but by the time they reached Hartshead Moor (quite possibly at the crossroads near Hartshead Church) it was dark and the snow lay thick.

The Luddites blindfolded the waggoners, tied them up, broke the frames to pieces and got away. Four men from Jackson's had carried out the attack; John Hirst, the undoubted leader of the Spen Valley Luddites, Jonas Crowther, Bob Whitwam and John Naylor.

It was at this point that the Government made machine breaking a capital offence but there were a further thirteen machine breaking incidents that February, 1812. And many late night raids by large bands of armed men searching for money and weapons.

These men became well organised, marching and drilling in military fashion, blackening their faces or sometimes whitening them and wearing disguises which might include women's clothing.

They generally attacked the rural areas around Huddersfield: the Colne Valley, the Holme Valley and here in the Spen Valley. Areas where they could attack or steal and slip away without being seen.

So far these Luddites had met with no opposition, but the authorities were now thoroughly alarmed.

The most hostile magistrate in the Huddersfield area was Joseph Radcliffe of Milnsbridge House, a prominent Colne Valley landowner who was aggressively engaged in repressing meetings and disturbances. Anyone seen as a possible threat was immediately dragged off to York prison.

But it was becoming increasingly impossible to use the existing law enforcement system of Watch and Ward because the local community's sympathies lay with the Luddites. This was in effect, a type of guerilla warfare.

A committee of magistrates and merchants was formed on February 23rd with John Horsfall (a millowner) as chairman. Instead of relying on a local militia made up from the community, and therefore likely to sympathise with the Luddites' situation, they decided to call in the army.

They were to protect the mills and the shearing frames but also the homes of the millowners. And the magistrates!

There were 12,000 troops assigned to deal with the Luddite threat throughout the Midlands, Lancashire and the West Riding of Yorkshire. This was a greater number than Wellington's army fighting in Spain!

It shows the extent to which the Government was prepared to go to prevent what they considered to be revolutionary activity. And how frightened they were by the developing situation.

In Huddersfield alone there were 1,000 soldiers billeted in the public houses but the isolated valleys around Huddersfield, like the Spen Valley, were hard to control.

George Mellor now wanted to increase the stakes and attack the mills, not just the machines. He particularly hated William Cartwright of Rawfolds and William Horsfall of Ottiwells Mill, in Marsden because they had ridiculed the Luddites and bragged about their defences against any attack Horsfall had even installed a cannon to protect his property! He persuaded his fellow Luddites to teach Cartwright a lesson.

Saturday, 11th of April was fixed for an attack on Rawfolds Mill. The plan was hatched at another cropper's inn St Crispins Inn in Halifax but the final details were made at The Shears Inn in Liversedge.

On the 11th April a Luddite messenger visited all the centres warning them to be ready. He arrived at Jackson's workshop just as the men were leaving for their dinner, and where he was spotted by William Fearnside.

Many of the men did not return to work that afternoon. They were in The Shears Inn listening to the details of the attack. It was arranged that they would assemble at night in the field near the Dumb Steeple which was on a crossroads which made it a central meeting place for the Huddersfield Luddites and the Spen Valley Luddites.

THE MARCH

On the night, Saturday the 11th April, George Mellor made a rousing speech and warned the throng of about one hundred and fifty men present that they were up against an armed defence and that it would take a lot of courage and determination to succeed.

William Hall who eventually appeared as a prosecution witness after changing sides said in his testament in court that, *'Before they left the field they called over the people, not by name but by number. There was a man who formed them into a line. There were two companies of pistol men. There was also a company of musket men, which marched first, then there were hatchetmen and others who had sticks or nothing at all.'*

At midnight they trooped off even though they were about fifty men short. Those leading the way were George Mellor, William Thorpe, James Haigh, John Walker and John Booth.

Samuel Hartley who was a cropper from Rawfolds mill was to act as guide. The two men who were appointed to drive the stragglers forward; William Hall and George Rigg saw a deserter slipping over the wall. He had taken fright at the last minute. This was a man called Rayner, but as he was a champion runner, he made it home to Brighouse in time to meet a local vicar who later gave testimony to the time that they spoke and this freed Rayner from suspicion!

They had three miles to march. They were meeting the Halifax Luddites at Rawfolds. We are not totally certain of the route they took but this is the most likely one:

From the field near the Dumb Steeple they went up Cross Hill Lane to Hartshead Lane, on to Church Lane and past Hartshead Church. They then crossed Peep Green Moor towards the Quaker graveyard and started down Upper House Lane (where another deserter slipped away). They then joined Clough Lane and on to Halifax Road.

The deserter was Nayler; one of the machine breakers, who lived in a cottage on Halifax Road opposite Jackson's cropping shop. (This cottage is still standing, in a little group of cottages next to Hightown Primary School).

Once they had crossed the fields and common, they were marching on roads.

Frank Peel describes the noise as the men marched down the highway. This wakened the sleeping householders who rushed to their windows where they glimpsed the army of men with their hatchets and hammers gleaming dimly in the starlight.

The men marched down Halifax Road and turned left down Primrose Lane and across the Spen bridge and there in front of them lay Rawfolds Mill.

THE ATTACK

Cartwright was well prepared.

He and five soldiers were sleeping at the mill. He could call on many more soldiers billeted just up Halifax Road in the barn at Thomas Greene's old house, Haigh House and at Millbridge and The George Inn in Cleckheaton. All the inns in Heckmondwike were brimming with soldiers.

He just had to ring the alarm bell. He had a heavy mill door studded with iron, and spiked rollers on the stairs. He had two tubs of vitriol (acid) ready to pour down and he could lift flagstones on the upper floor to make a parapet from which to fire down on to the Luddites.

The Luddites themselves were armed. Those marching at the front, under Mellor, carried guns. Thorpe led the next group, carrying pistols. The rest carried only hatchets, hammers and hedge stakes or were without weapons at all. There was no sign of the Halifax Luddites who should have met them here.

The attackers overpowered the two night watchmen and tied them up and smashed down the mill gates, but their attempts to break down the mill door failed. By now the garrison was on full alert and muskets were pointed down on the mill yard ready for the command to open fire. The Luddites threw stones up at the windows, smashing them and then fired a volley through the empty windows.

Frank Peel depicted the events, as the silent building suddenly erupted with the sound of musket fire echoing sharply through the valley. ·

The Leeds Mercury described the scene that followed, *'The fire from within was kept up with so much steadiness and perseverance.'* and, *'one hundred and forty musket ball were discharged.'*

The rioters continued to try and break down the mill door, and the noise of the hammers mixed with the clanging of the alarm bell. The door would not yield and the situation for the Luddites was getting desperate. After a twenty minute gun battle their meagre ammunition was exhausted and the soldiers would soon be on the scene.

Several men were wounded; two of them so badly that they had to be left in the mill yard when Mellor and his men were finally forced to flee, leaving the yard strewn with hammers, axes, keys, pick locks, bullet moulds and other debris on the blood-stained ground. Everything had gone wrong. An organised group of men had turned into a terrified rabble; rushing to escape.

THE AFTERMATH

Most retreated in the direction of Huddersfield but others fled across the Spen river and up towards Hightown and down to Clifton and then on to Brighouse.

In this flight, is an interesting little story linking back to the deserter, Naylor, who had stolen away to his bed.

He was naturally ill at ease and kept getting up and going outside where he saw the flashes of light down in the valley. Mrs. Fearnside, wife of the foreman at Jacksons, saw him and knowing what was happening, she demanded he went back to bed. It was just as well, because his wife didn't know anything about the events of the night, and when some of the escaping Luddites rapped on her door she let them in.

Thomas Brook had fallen into the mill goit and lost his hat and they had called to borrow one for him as it was suspicious to be seen without a hat (a bareheaded man in Regency England would have drawn attention to himself).

Naylor's wife lent him one but when the soldiers found the hat in the mill goit, they realised who it belonged to because Mrs. Naylor, being a great one for gossip, told the story of her midnight encounter to anyone who would listen. Poor Brook was apprehended and Mrs. Naylor gave evidence against him.

Apparently her husband refused to live with her afterwards! Thomas Brooke was one of the men hanged at York.

And what about the two badly injured men left behind? They were Samuel Hartley and John Booth.

According to the Leeds Mercury,

'Hartley had received a shot in his left breast which passed through his body lodged beneath the skin at the left shoulder from whence it was extracted with a portion of the bone. In this situation he languished until 3 o'clock on Monday morning. Booth's wound was in his leg, which was shattered almost to atoms; it was found necessary that he should have his leg amputated, but owing to the extreme loss of blood before the surgeon arrived, spasms came on during the operation and he died about 6 o'clock on Sunday morning.'

Both men had been carried from the scene to The Yew Tree Inn (now Headlands Hall) but when a large and sympathetic crowd gathered, the military removed the men to The Star Inn in Roberttown where the crowds had to be held back by cavalrymen.

Some say they were tortured by the application of strong acid to their wounds while being interrogated by the military.

It is said that Cartwright's friend, the Rev. Hammond Roberson, tried to get them to inform on their fellow Luddites and that as he lay dying Booth signalled to Roberson to come to his side,

'*Can you keep a secret?*' gasped the dying man, '*I can,*' eagerly replied the expectant clergyman, '*So can I...*' replied poor Booth and calmly died.

Star Inn, Roberttown

On April 15th 1812, the funeral of Sam Hartley was held in Halifax. There were huge crowds, all in mourning. The authorities were so worried that when John Booth was buried in Huddersfield, the following day, they changed the time from noon to 6 o'clock. This angered the Luddites, particularly George Mellor, even more.

MURDER

There were several attacks on mills but the attack on Rawfolds proved a turning point. Machine breaking had been abandoned in favour of reprisals on millowners and magistrates and the seizure of arms which some historians consider was the prelude to an uprising.

This is at the heart of the question, debated ever since. Were the Luddites rebels or revolutionaries?

Mellor vowed to kill the millowners who were gloating at their success. Soon after the funerals of Hartley and Booth, Cartwright was shot at but escaped. There were two other abortive shootings, then on April 28th William Horsfall, the millowner who Mellor hated the most, was mortally wounded as he returned to his home in Marsden from the Cloth Hall in Huddersfield.

The four men allegedly involved in the murder were George Mellor, William Thorpe, Thomas Smith and Benjamin Walker. They had lain in wait for Horsfall as he rode his horse over Crosland Moor.

Another horseman on the road that day, Henry Parr, testified at the trial of the four men that he heard shots and saw Horsfall slump on to his horse's neck and that he saw; *'Four persons in the plantation (wood) from which I was about one hundred and fifty yards'.*

Horsfall had bragged that he would ride up to his saddle in Luddite blood, but it was his own blood that was lost that day and it was his death that really led to the end of the Yorkshire Luddites.

The cause now lost a lot of support from the local community and the authorities stepped up their investigations. The whole area was put under martial law.

There was heightened tension throughout the North of England. There were rumours that Napoleon Bonaparte had 10,000 troops standing by for invasion. The Spen Valley area received a massive allocation of troops many of which were encamped at Millbridge from where they began the task of tracking down those who had broken the law in such a spectacular fashion.

In May, illegal oath taking was made a capital offence and in July magistrates were given much wider powers under Watch and Ward. They were now empowered to enter premises in search of weapons and crucially they were able to grant a free pardon to those confessing offences and those turning King's evidence. There were still many soldiers stationed in the Huddersfield area throughout the summer, but by August, order was gradually being restored.

TRIAL AND PUNISHMENT

The authorities rounded up more than a hundred men from the area. Sixty four were charged and taken to York Castle where they were to await trial. They were all treated as Luddites but there was a variety of charges; very many were arraigned on charges of theft. This was to be a show trial by means of which the Government would warn against any further trouble.

The planning for the trial began in May but by September it was postponed so as to get as much evidence as possible to avoid any of the prisoners being acquitted.

In the event, more than thirty were never brought to trial. They were discharged on bail; even though there was no evidence against them. For the rest, their alibis were totally ignored and they continued to suffer in the dark damp cells of York Castle.

It was not until the autumn that Benjamin Walker broke the Luddite oath and betrayed the other three Luddites who had murdered William Horsfall. Mellor, Thorpe and Smith were arrested and taken to York Castle to join the others. William Hall, the man who had introduced Luddism into the Spen Valley in the first place, also turned King's evidence and saved himself from the death penalty. But he never divulged the identity of John Hirst, the leader of the Spen Valley Luddites.

In January 1813, the trial of the three men accused of murder began. It was a foregone conclusion. They were sent to the gallows thirty six hours after their conviction so that there would be no time for an appeal. At 9am on the 9th of January, Mellor, Thorpe and Smith were taken behind the Castle wall. Two troops of cavalry were drawn up in front of the gallows and the entrances to the Castle were guarded by the infantry.

All three men prayed aloud and the crowd of onlookers were very affected by their prayers. Normally, by the standards of 1813, public hangings were considered to be great entertainment but this was very different. The atmosphere was funereal and the crowds sang hymns and prayed.

It was now the turn of the others. Fourteen of the men were condemned to death; five for riot and attempt to demolish William Cartright's watermill, six for burglary and three for robbery. Fourteen others were to be transported to the colonies, six of them for receiving illegal oaths. Only seven were acquitted.

On the 16th January the fourteen men were executed by the York hangman, John Curry. It was York's biggest ever hanging. They were hanged in two groups; one group at 11 am and the other at 1.30 pm. This was made possible by the invention of the New Drop a new type of gallows. There were large crowds but the horse and foot soldiers before and behind the scaffold gave the appearance of a military execution, making it clear that the men were being hanged for political reasons. Again the crowds were quiet and respectful as they joined in prayers and hymn singing.

The hanging of 17 men sent a clear signal to the workers of the Spen Valley. The authorities had got the upper hand and Luddism was dead. By March 1813, the bulk of the militia was withdrawn from Yorkshire.

There is a story that among the graves in the old part of Hartshead Church are those of Luddites who were buried secretly by night; in the south- east corner of the churchyard, nearest the road.

There was a lot of secrecy in the area at this time. And fear. There was also continued deprivation especially among the families of those most affected by the recent troubles. Sixty six children were orphaned and families were left broken and often homeless.

In the Spring of 1812, two Quakers, Thomas Shillitoe and Joseph Wood embarked on a journey around the Huddersfield area visiting the families of the Luddites. It is the only real insight we have into the very real distress which was being suffered. Only the Quakers could have done this. The Anglicans opposed the Luddites and the Methodists worried about getting involved for fear of reprisals.

They sat with the widows and children and the parents of the Luddites and prayed with them. They reported very poignant scenes such as the widow left with seven children, *'She appeared in a very tryed state both inwardly and outwardly.'*

They met the parents of William Hartley who had taken in his eight children, his wife having died eight months before his execution for robbery. Several of their neighbours saw them arrive and they joined them and, *'Sat down quietly with us.'*

They also visited the home of the informer Benjamin Walker and not surprisingly found he had moved house and was living with his parents who had also had to move house! They found him in a very bad state but were able to, *'Open a door of utterance and give him such advice as to tend for his future peace.'*

William Cartwright on the other hand became a local hero in some quarters. The local millowners rewarded him with the staggering sum of three thousand pounds with which he not only bought his rented mill but enlarged it.

Chief Magistrate, Joseph Radcliffe was given a Baronetcy for his role in repressing the uprising. The croppers for their part, set up a fund to support those who had been wounded at Rawfolds, and their families.

Luddism might be dead, but the spirit of radicalism lived on.

The working classes continued to oppose mills and machinery and eventually became involved in the Plug Riots in the 1840's. They also rioted against the Government when it introduced the Workhouse System and they banded together to demand the vote for the working classes.

Since those first short months in 1812, however, Britain has never come so close to civil war and revolution. The events of 1812 were a dramatic ending to a country-wide outbreak of machine-breaking and lawlessness. But the actual word Luddite did not disappear. It has never left the English Language and is still familiar across the English speaking world. It is most often used as a term of abuse for anyone with a fear of technological progress.

However most Luddites did not oppose innovations as such, but the circumstances of their use. They were against the use of new machinery by the controllers of land and capital i.e. the millowners and their friends making a profit at the expense of themselves and their fellow workers.

Many of them were so desperate that they felt that violent protest was the only way they could exert control over the changes taking place; changes which had occurred at the same time as terrible economic hardship.

No-one was listening to them. No one in authority was helping them.

They were simply left with no hope in a fast changing world.

Charlotte Bronte gives the best description of their motives in her book 'Shirley.'

She explains about the war with France closing down export markets and says, at the same time,

'Certain inventions in machinery were introduced into the staple manufacture of the North, which greatly reduced the amount of hands necessary to be employed, threw thousands out of work and left them without legitimate means of sustaining life.'

She acknowledged the fact that there was no other avenue to express their feelings of hopelessness and she understood their discontent full well when she says,

'Misery generates hate. These sufferers hated the machines which they believed took their bread from them; they hated the buildings which contained those machines and they hated the manufacturers who owned those buildings.'

But the Luddites were fighting more than just inventions in the textile industry. They were fighting the 'system.' The landed aristocracy who ruled the country, were terrified of a French-style Revolution.

There was no pretence that they shared any common ground with the working classes. The draconian laws against the workers forming unions forced the Luddites to become more secretive, more organised and more and more violent.

There was one member of the aristocracy, however, who understood their plight.

And that was the poet, Lord Byron…

Lord Byron

Byron was a great champion of the Luddite Cause. He saw at first hand how the workers of Nottinghamshire were suffering. In his maiden speech on February 27th 1812, he joined in the debate about how the Government was to deal with them. The discussion was whether machine breaking was a capital offence.

He pleaded on the Luddites' behalf that their actions,

'Have arisen from circumstances of the most unparalleled distress - nothing but absolute want could have driven a large and once honest and industrious body of people into excesses so hazardous to themselves, their families and the community.'

He points to the successes in the fight against Napoleon Bonaparte,

'But all the cities you have taken, all the armies which have retreated before your leaders, are but paltry subjects of self congratulation if your land divides itself and your dragoons must be let loose against your fellow citizens.' and continues, *'With what alacrity you fly to the succour of your distressed allies leaving the distressed of your own country to the care of the parish.'*

On the subject of the punishment of the Luddites, which their Lordships were debating, he asked,

'Will you erect a gibbet in every field and hang up men like scarecrows? Are these the remedies for a starving and desperate populace? Will the famished wretch who has braved your bayonets be appalled by your gibbets? When death is a relief will he be dragooned into tranquility? If you proceed by law where is your evidence? Those who have refused to impeach their accomplices when transportation only was the punishment will hardly be tempted to witness against them when death is the penalty.'

Lord Byron concluded this speech with the following opinion,

'Suppose it passed; suppose one of these men as I have seen them - meagre with famine, sullen with despair, careless of a life which your Lordships are perhaps to value at something less than the price of a stocking frame - suppose this man surrounded by the children for whom he is unable to procure bread, at the hazard of his existence, about to be torn for ever from a family which he lately supported in peaceful industry and which it is not his fault that he can no longer support - suppose this man and there are ten thousand such from whom you may select your victims, dragged into court to be tried for this new offence by this law, still there are two things wanting to convict and condemn him, and these are in my opinion, twelve butchers for a jury and a Jefferies for a Judge.'

(a reference to a notoriously wicked judge)

Byron startled his fellow peers by his attitude but, despite his passionate speech, the Bill was passed and the Act which followed led to the harshest of measures against the Luddites throughout industrial England.

This Act of Parliament of 20th March 1812 was the Frame Breaking Act which said that anyone accused of machine breaking would be sentenced to death. As a further precaution, the Government ordered 12,000 troops into the areas where the Luddites were active. We have now seen the consequences of this for the men of Huddersfield and the Spen Valley whose actions so troubled the Tory government of the day.

Despite a national strategy for dealing with unrest, those responsible locally for the maintenance of law and order were extremely worried. The Chief Magistrate of the area, Joseph Radcliffe wrote to the Home Office,

'Having been told by several friends that I am one of them marked for destruction I trust to your goodness in affording me a guard of ten privates and an officer to be here day and night - in two rooms adjoining my stables.'

The merchants and millowners also felt a very real sense of threat.

It was hardly surprising that the 'establishment' associated machine breaking with activity of a more political nature in the light of all that was going on in the year 1812.

However it was the new machinery in the finishing trade which was the major cause of Luddism in the West Riding of Yorkshire although the multitude of other pressures gave the croppers more resolve.

In other parts of the country, machine breaking was linked to other causes, for example the fight for better working conditions.

On the 11th May, the Prime Minister was assassinated! Spencer Percival was shot at point-blank range through the chest as he entered the lobby of the House of Commons. This had absolutely nothing to do with Luddism. It was the act of a man who had a grievance and who felt no-one in authority had listened to him.

Not surprisingly there was a level of public sympathy for him but not for the Prime Minister!

The Leeds Mercury however, writing for a middle class readership, worried that, *'We are much concerned that the death of the Prime Minister has not been received with the abhorrence that deeds of this nature should call for.'*

But the immediate result of the whole Luddite episode was that the 'establishment' had made some progress in recovering a position it had long ago lost.

We can still see sites associated with the Luddite disturbances. Near the site of Rawfolds mill there is still a street named Cartwright Street and William Cartwright's grave is in Liversedge churchyard.

To mark the bi-centenary of the Luddites, the Spen Valley Civic Society has built a commemorative park at the junction of Knowler Hill and Halifax Road.

It includes a statue of a cropper and his child.

The Luddite Memorial, Liversedge

The message of the memorial is that the workers were fighting for their families' survival. They had to take desperate measures.

After 1815 and the end of the Napoleonic War the economy slowly staring to recover, but more problems lay ahead...

FURTHER UNREST AND AGITATION

RIOTS IN 1837-1838 AGAINST THE NEW POOR LAW

The early years of the 19th Century saw the emergence of a new class of people; the Working Class, but as we have seen from the experiences of the Luddites, these labourers were suffering terrible poverty. The old system of charity simply could not cope with poverty on such a scale.

In 1834, a new Poor Law Act abolished the old system of poor relief which had been started in Queen Elizabeth I reign and the old small workhouses at Gomersal, Heckmondwike, White Lee and Roberttown were closed down. Instead, the Dewsbury Poor Law Union was formed and the Staincliffe Institute was built to take in all the destitute people from a wide area. This was on the site of the present Dewsbury District Hospital at Staincliffe, Dewsbury.

This large establishment, like all the other workhouses built at this time throughout the country, was made as harsh and unwelcoming as possible. Workhouses were hated by the poor. They were regarded as little better than prisons and the dread of being thrown into the workhouse was a constant fear.

It was felt that this New Poor Law marked the breaking of the last bond which had once bound the poor of the community to the richer classes.

The last link had gone in the way poverty had always been dealt with i.e. the rich helping the poor at the time help was needed. Religious dissenters were particularly badly treated.

And there were still an awful lot of those in the Spen Valley.

Riots broke out in Dewsbury because that's where the new headquarters for the Poor Law administration now existed. But local radicals from the Spen Valley eagerly joined in.

CHARTISM

Chartism was a national movement started in London with the object of reforming Parliament.

The main demands were to get the vote for every man and woman in the country and to make the electoral districts fairer, so as to meet the new demographic distribution brought about by the Industrial Revolution. It was borne out of the need for ordinary working-class people being represented in Parliament and getting their voices heard.

But when the Reform Act was passed, in 1832, it only enfranchised the middle classes (so the working classes still had no vote) and it did not address the real problems of electoral distribution (so the spread of constituencies did not reflect the spread of population). This meant that political agitation continued. A People's Charter was drawn up.

The people fighting for this particular cause were called Chartists.

The people of Liversedge and Heckmondwike were very much to the fore in this radical movement. They even set up Chartist Chapels where meetings took on the character of a service.

The Chartist meetings were mainly held however, in the inns, like The Black Bull in Millbridge and The Yew Tree (now Headlands Hall) in Liversedge.

It was at the latter that a group of delegates from Liversedge, Heckmondwike and Cleckheaton, decided to organise a demonstration at Peep Green Common (between Roberttown and Hartshead) on Whit Monday, 1839.

There had been other Chartist meetings on Peep Green Common and on Castle Hill, but this was going to be the 'big one.'

Frank Peel described what happened, as thousands of people gathered from all parts of the West Riding. He said it was a sight that those present would never forget. There were brass bands, flag waving and banners proclaiming their cause. The crowd's enthuiasm was infectious.

What he does not mention were the Government spies looking for weapons and any sign of revolution, but despite feelings running high, there was no major disorder. The enthusiastic cheering must have been deafening when the leading spokesman, Feargus O'Connor stood up to speak.

There were estimated to be a quarter of a million people in that crowd. Some came from outside the West Riding. One of the groups, led by a brass band, marched all the way from Todmorden. It is said to have been the largest ever open-air political meeting in British history!

And it took place right here in what is still known as the Chartists' Fields.

Chartist's Fields, Roberttown

These fields were in fact at that time part of Peep Green Common which was open moorland where everyone had access.

Three years after this event the authorities decided to have the Commons enclosed. This denied access to the area and ensured no such meetings would ever again be possible.

New roads were built across the former commons; Peep Green Road, School Lane and Prospect Road.

The working classes in the Spen Valley were foiled again.

THE PLUG RIOTS

Class tensions in many parts of England were so inflammable in the 1840's (as they were all over Europe) that the Government feared revolution yet again.

The Plug Riots were part of the Chartist movement. Political agitators encouraged action against the millowners. It was thought that by drawing the plugs from the boilers in the mills, they would force the mills to stop production and bring the country to its knees.

The movement had started in Lancashire and moved to Halifax and on to the Spen Valley where it found support from everywhere except Cleckheaton where the inhabitants were not quite so radical.

In fact they put the town in a state of defence and prepared to send for the soldiers stationed at Bradford! There was still no police force and therefore only one constable available to protect all the mills.

On 16th August 1842 a group attacked George Anderton's mill in Cleckheaton, but were driven back by the workers there. Two days later, a huge throng of workers marched again. This time there were estimated to have been five to six thousand desperate men and women.

Frank Peel talks about the army of men with their weaponry; bludgeons, flails, pitchforks and pikes, with coarse grey blankets strapped to their backs. They surged down the hillside in their hundreds. They seemed to Peel a gaunt famished looking desperate multitude. Many had no coats or hats and they resembled scarecrows, with their clothes in rags and tatters.

They approached Roundhill Mill and drew the plugs without any opposition. They then went on to St Peg's Mill where they pulled two of the three plugs before the alarm was raised. By this time, the soldiers had arrived from Leeds and Bradford and several hundred special constables had been sworn in (nearly every man in the town).

The rioters were not to be deterred and started throwing stones at the mounted soldiers. The soldiers retaliated by firing into the crowd and followed this up by riding into the throng and striking out with their sabres.

There was fierce fighting and eventually the crowd panicked and fled but not before the special constables had made their arrests. These included three Gomersal men; Charles Leighton, a farmer; Richard Thomson, a clothier and Thomas Barber, a collier, as well as another collier, John Hey from Hightown.

According to Peel, twenty to thirty rioters were taken into custody but not before the hillsides around were black with wild struggling masses of people trying to escape from the horsemen who rode after them flourishing their weapons.

The Plug riots were at an end! And with them there was an end to violent political action in the Spen Valley.

But this period of history, here as in the rest of the country, was an important milestone in the working man's struggle for equality and democracy.

CHAPTER 8 : CHARLOTTE BRONTE IN THE SPEN VALLEY

There was one person who knew all about the Spen Valley, as she spent so much of her life here. And that was Charlotte Bronte.

PATRICK BRONTE

In fact it was her father, Patrick Bronte who first came to live in the area.

He came from Ireland at the age of thirty-two and became curate at Dewsbury Parish Church assisting the Reverend John Buckworth. In his two years in Dewsbury, he made a name for himself as a great advocate of Sunday Schools.

The Sunday School system in Dewsbury is one of the oldest in the country. It was established in 1783, by the Reverend Hammond Roberson, only three years after Robert Raikes set up the very first sunday school in England. Roberson had helped these schools to flourish throughout the Dewsbury area and Patrick Bronte (who succeeded Roberson) continued this work.

On 22nd July, 1811, Patrick Bronte became Curate at Hartshead Church. He proved to be a very caring minister. His style of Anglicanism was such that he embraced the teachings of Wesley and worked for the benefit of the poor in his Parish. He lodged with a Mr. and Mrs. Bedford at nearby Thornbush Farm (which can still be seen from Windy Bank Lane). While there, he wrote books, visited Kirklees Hall, in a social capacity, and he also became a School Inspector.

On one of his inspections, he visited Woodhouse Grove School at Rawdon with his old friend the Reverend William Morgan. Woodhouse Grove was an academy for the sons of Wesleyan Ministers. Morgan was engaged to the headmaster's daughter, Jane Fennel. It so happened that her cousin, Maria Branwell had arrived from Cornwall and she caught the eye of Patrick.

Maria was the eighth of eleven children born into a prosperous merchant family who were the leading members of the Wesleyan Methodist Church of Penzance.

Four deaths between 1808 and 1811, including her mother and father, meant that Maria had to seek employment. Her father's sister was the wife of the Headmaster at Woodhouse Grove School and he offered her the post of housekeeper.

After a brief courtship, (Maria only arrived in Yorkshire in the summer of 1812) and a proposal in the grounds of Kirkstall Abbey (to which they walked on the day of their betrothal!)

Patrick and Maria were married at Guiseley Church on the 29th December 1812. It was a double wedding with the Morgans. The two clergymen performed the ceremonies for each other.

There is a double wedding at the end of Charlotte Bronte's novel 'Shirley.' Charlotte obviously liked this particular kind of happy ending.

THE BRONTE FAMILY

In 1813, Patrick Bronte brought his bride to live in the tall three-storied 18th Century Clough House that he rented at the top of Clough Lane in Hightown, a mile from the Hartshead Church.

At the end of 1813, Maria was born and she was christened by the Reverend Morgan at Hartshead Church in April 1814.

A second daughter, Elizabeth, was born in Hightown in 1815, but she was christened at Thornton where the family went to live next.

In April 1816, Charlotte was born; the following year her brother Patrick Branwell was born, followed by Emily in 1818. Anne's birth in January 1820 completed the family.

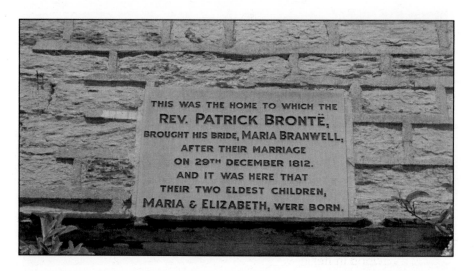

Clough House Hightown, Liversedge

Then in 1820 the Brontes went to live in Haworth where Patrick had been given a perpetual living.

After the birth of Anne, Maria Bronte's health began to decline. She was 29 years old when she married, which was old to be child-bearing for those times and over a period of seven years she had borne six children. By February 1820 when she first arrived at her new home, the Parsonage in Howarth, surrounded by its bleak moors, she was a sick woman. The children, all under the age of seven, had to be solemn and silent as their mother lay ill in her bedroom.

Maria died in February 1821 at the age of thirty-eight. The lives of her children became sadder and lonelier still. Charlotte never really remembered her. She was only four years old when her mother died.

Their mother's sister, Aunt Branwell, came from Cornwall to look after the family. The six children remained isolated from society but happy with their own company. They didn't have formal lessons but in July 1824, Patrick Bronte took his eldest two daughters to a boarding school at Cowan Bridge, on the coach-road between Leeds and Kendal. He thought he was giving them the opportunity of a good education.

It was a school that was subsidised by philanthropists because clergymen were not usually wealthy. However, money here was obviously in very short supply as the school (in an old disused mill) was badly organised, there was poor sanitation and unwholesome food.

In the autumn they were joined by Charlotte and Emily. In the spring of 1825, after suffering a harsh winter there, first Maria then Elizabeth died from a fever that was spreading throughout the school.

Charlotte and Emily were brought home but Charlotte was haunted by this great tragedy and she painted a vivid picture of life at Cowan Bridge naming it Lowood in her novel Jane Eyre. It is a heart- rending description of what happened to her sisters.

CHARLOTTE BRONTE AT ROE HEAD SCHOOL

Patrick Bronte would no doubt be devastated by the deaths of his beloved daughters so soon after that of their mother but he did want his children to have an education.

He decided to send Charlotte to a school in his former parish of Hartshead. This was Roe Head which still stands on Far Common Road (at the time this was the main road from Leeds to Huddersfield) at Roberttown. It is still a school but now it looks after young people with severe physical disabilities.

Elizabeth Gaskell, Charlotte's biographer and contemporary, visited the Spen Valley and she described Roe Head. She talked about the position it held on the hillside and how through the bow windows you could see the parkland of Sir George Armytage which was full of history being the place where the ruins of Kirklees Priory and the grave of Robin Hood were situated. She thought the landscape was delightful.

Roe Head School, Roberttown

In January 1831, Charlotte arrived at Roe Head and although painfully shy, she soon became friends with the two girls who remained her closest friends throughout her life. They were Mary Taylor and Ellen Nussey. In fact there were only ten pupils at the school and five teachers. It was more like a private family home than a school.

Margaret Wooler was the head teacher. She was a good story teller and on long walks in the Spen Valley she related stories about Robin Hood and Kirklees Priory. She told her pupils about this old house or that new mill and she told them the story of the Luddites and of their mysterious late night manoeuvres on the lonely moors; of the muttered threats of men who had been greatly oppressed.

Her stories struck deep into the minds of at least one of her pupils. Charlotte had no doubt been told the story by her father as he was living at Thornbush Farm at the time of the Luddite attack and may even have heard the men as they marched past to Rawfolds Mill.

Charlotte worked hard to catch up with her hitherto meagre learning. She had a strong conviction of the necessity and value of education. She found it difficult to relax and was always studying, but one of her greatest skills was in story telling. At night when the girls lay in bed, she had them enthralled by the stories she made up, on more than one occasion making them scared out of their wits!

Charlotte would no doubt have been surprised at the different attitudes of the people of the Spen Valley as opposed to Haworth. There she would have been used to the respectful manners of the working class towards her family. Here there was greater freedom shown by workers to those above them.

Her experiences here were fresh and new. She was a Tory and a clergyman's daughter, used to talking about politics from a certain point of view. She was now living in a place where the bulk of the population were religious dissenters.

For example, nearby Heckmondwike had two large Independent Chapels and one Methodist Church all of which were completely filled two or three times each Sunday.

Mrs. Gaskell describes Heckmondwike at this time, '*A large straggling, dirty village principally inhabited by blanket weavers who worked in their own cottages. They had a heap of coal on one side of the house door and brewing tubs on the other*'

She thought Gomersal was a much prettier place.

MARY TAYLOR

Gomersal was the home of Mary Taylor and her younger sister Martha who was also a pupil at Roe Head.

We are well acquainted with the Taylors who lived at Red House. Their father, Joshua Taylor had the mill at Hunsworth where he made his army cloths as well as fine cloth which he exported to Europe. Charlotte based her story of the Luddite attack in 'Shirley' on this mill and not Rawfolds. Because she knew it so well.

Charlotte Bronte loved to visit Mary's home. It is now a museum, presented to the public as it would have looked when she visited, so it is easily recognised as Briarmains, the Yorke family home in 'Shirley.'

She found the company of the Taylor family exhilarating and their way of life very different from her own. They were very modern and radical in their ideas compared to the more conservative, Anglican regime at Haworth. The house was full of laughter and argument and noise. A world away from the routines of parsonage life.

She particularly admired Joshua Taylor who became Hiram Yorke in her book. And with some justification. Joshua Taylor had a considerable influence on Charlotte Bronte.

He was well educated and encouraged her to read French literature and he supplied her with books. He was well travelled and spoke fluent French and Italian because of his business trips to the Continent. He had a great love of art and music as well as literature which he talked about to Charlotte. But above all, he had radical views on politics and religion and he encouraged his family, (four sons and two daughters) to discuss the issues of the day. Once she got used to it, Charlotte enjoyed the noisy arguments and discussions that filled the house.

Mary Taylor was Charlotte's age and she was strong minded like her father. While they were at school, Mary was always persuading Charlotte to be more assertive and independent. She was very out-going and gregarious.

After leaving Roe Head, Mary enjoyed travelling on the Continent. She studied in Brussels, taught at a boys school in Germany and in 1848 she settled in New Zealand (where her brother had emigrated) where she set up a shop. She had tried to persuade Charlotte to go with her but she couldn't leave Haworth and her father because of his ill health.

This was a very unconventional life for a young woman. But it was also an inspiration and driving force for Charlotte. It was Mary Taylor who urged Charlotte to further her education so that she and her sisters could be qualified to run their own school one day. It was through her that Charlotte and Emily went to Brussels to study. This provided the experiences on which her novels Villette and The Professor were based. Charlotte's writing gained from her life in Brussels, especially her frustrated love for her (married) tutor.

Mary was an early feminist and thought women should support themselves and not be financially dependent on their husbands and fathers. Charlotte was influenced enough to touch on this subject in her novels, but in her letters from New Zealand, Mary criticized her for being too half hearted on women's rights, appearing to argue for the right of women to work but only for unmarried women.

Mary, on the other hand, wrote feminist articles for a national magazine and published three books in her lifetime. She was an early pioneer in the hard fought battle for women's rights. She refused to accept restrictions on women and in her books and pamphlets she urged women to win their independence.

It is not always recognised how important Joshua Taylor and his daughter Mary were in shaping Charlotte's ideas and philosophy.

Before she left England for New Zealand, Mary had a very emotional parting with Charlotte. This was to be the last time the two great friends would meet. Charlotte died in 1855 and Mary only returned to England in 1861.

She settled back in Gomersal, at High Royd which she had built (on Taylor land) and where she died of a stroke in 1893. High Royd is now the Gomersal Lodge Hotel, on Spen Lane.

In a letter to Ellen Nussey September 1844, Charlotte wrote, '*Mary Taylor is going to leave our hemisphere - to me it is something as if a great planet fell out of the sky.*'

Elizabeth Gaskell was Charlotte's first biographer but she only knew Charlotte personally for the last four and a half years of her life and therefore the basis of her biography is largely drawn from correspondence. This means that there is very little written evidence about Mary Taylor and her father.

And obviously after Mary emigrated to New Zealand, her influence on Charlotte waned. But the fact that Mary destroyed Charlotte's letters meant that Mrs. Gaskell had no real understanding of the influences of the family at Red House. Despite not seeing Charlotte for eleven years, Mary corresponded regularly and as usual passed on her advice and opinions. But the letters she received from Charlotte she considered private and that is why she destroyed them.

ELLEN NUSSEY

Ellen Nussey, on the other hand, emerges as one of the main sources of the biography. She allowed Mrs. Gaskell to read all her letters from Charlotte.

Ellen Nussey was Charlotte's other close school friend from her schooldays at Roe Head. She lived at the Rydings Hall in Birstall. (the old Popeley Hall) Her family were County, rather than tradespeople. Ellen's brother was court physician and they were a more genteel family than the Taylors.

Charlotte loved visiting here and on one occasion, Branwell Bronte accompanied his sister in the Haworth gig. He stayed to look around and when he left, he said he was, *'Leaving her in paradise.'*

The Rydings Hall, Birstall

The house had been re-built in the 18th Century and has a battlemented roof. It was at the time surrounded by parkland.

It is still just visible from the A62 road near Birstall Smithies. But the main road now cuts right through the former parkland. And the house itself is surrounded by factory buildings.

This was the setting for another of Charlotte's novels, Jane Eyre. She calls the house Thornfield Hall and describes Ellen's home in great detail in her book. Ellen's father, Henry Nussey provided Charlotte with the character of St John Rivers in Jane Eyre.

She says of the house; *'It is a gentleman's manor house; battlements round the top give it a picturesque look.'*

Ellen moved from the Rydings and went to live in Brookroyd House, also in Birstall. Charlotte visited Ellen here and while sitting in the garden, she looked over the proofs of Jane Eyre. This was in the summer of 1847. This house too still exists as does Ellen's last home which was in Moor Lane, Gomersal. This is now the Gomersal Park Hotel. Ellen died in 1897, aged 80, and is buried in the churchyard in Birstall, the church which Charlotte calls Briarfield in 'Shirley.'

It became easier to send letters in 1840 with the introduction of the Penny Post and Charlotte and Ellen certainly took full advantage of it. Charlotte's letters were very relaxed and gossipy to Ellen. She might have written differently had she known that these letters would be used after her death.

Ellen Nussey preserved all her letters from Charlotte and these provided Mrs. Gaskell with a wealth of detail about her life. Mary Taylor was horrified by this. She thought that Ellen's action in giving up this information was a betrayal of Charlotte's privacy and the two became estranged in later life.

Ellen Nussey's relationship with Charlotte was different from but by no means less significant than her relationship with Mary Taylor. Ellen was a gentle, sensitive girl and Charlotte looked on her as a sister.

Charlotte often visited both her friends in the school holidays and when she returned to Roe Head as a teacher in 1835, she was delighted to be close to them again. This time Emily enrolled as a pupil at Roe Head and Charlotte paid her fees from her own salary of £16 a year.

At about this time an event happened which caused a good deal of interest in the Spen Valley. A governess had been wooed and married to a gentleman and they had a child, then soon after it was discovered that he already had a wife. The excuse he gave for his behaviour was that his first wife was deranged. Just one of the local stories which Charlotte stored in her memory. It next surfaced as an integral part of the plot of 'Jane Eyre.'

Emily hated living away from Haworth and her place at the school was taken by Anne. Then in 1838, Charlotte left Roe Head and became a governess. She held two posts; in 1838 at Lothersdale for three months and in 1839 at Rawdon for nine months.

Emily also took a Governess's post at Law Hill, in Halifax, which only lasted six months and Anne worked as governess for nine months at Blake Hall in Mirfield and a staggering five years in York! Anne was the only one of the Bronte Sisters who managed to really make the tedious job of being a governess actually work.

But all three sisters resented teaching and Charlotte's letters to Ellen are full of grumbles. They regarded their work teaching the sons and daughters of the newly successful millowners as sheer drudgery. Their big plan was to start a school of their own at the Parsonage. Charlotte was familiar with such schools as another friend from Roe Head, Elizabeth Cockhill, helped her mother and sisters run a boarding school at Oakwell Hall. Charlotte, Mary and Ellen often visited her there.

In order to acquire the language skills which would attract more pupils to their school, Charlotte and Emily spent a year in Brussels, in 1842, at the Pensionnat Heger funded by their Aunt Branwell. They chose this academy as Mary and Martha Taylor were studying there.

They had to return home later that year when their Aunt died. Emily stayed behind to look after their father while Charlotte returned for another eighteen months.

Martha Taylor's sudden death in Brussels is portrayed in an episode in 'Shirley,' and after Mary left, Charlotte was incredibly lonely and wrote asking Ellen if she could join her.

After 1844, Charlotte remained at Haworth. The school project foundered and the three sisters began writing novels. Ellen Nussey visited them in August 1847 and though curious about the books, said nothing.

From this time onwards, Charlotte depended on Ellen's letters and on brief visits to Ellen's home in Birstall more and more. Her father's ill health and her brother Branwell's moral and physical decline were a great worry to her. In September 1848, Branwell died (probably of tuberculosis) aged thirty one.

Three months later Emily died of tuberculosis, aged twenty nine. Anne was sickening with the same disease and Charlotte and her father were distraught. The Nussey family proposed she should come and stay with them in Scarborough to try and help her to recover.

Ellen and Charlotte were with her in May of 1849 when Anne died, aged twenty nine. To spare her father attending yet another funeral, Charlotte arranged for her to be buried in St Mary's churchyard in Scarborough.

Throughout this terrible period, Charlotte was writing 'Shirley.' Its no wonder that she calls one of her chapters, *'The Valley of the Shadow of Death.'*

This book sustained her through her grief. The nine months that she was writing 'Shirley' must have been the worst of her life. The two poems that she wrote on the death of each of her sisters are some of the most poignant in the English Language.

In 1854 she was engaged to be married to her father's curate, Arthur Bell Nicholls and in June of that year, they were married. Miss Wooler gave the bride away and Ellen Nussey was her bridesmaid. Her happiness was short-lived.

Charlotte died in the early stages of pregnancy on the 31st March 1855. She was thirty eight years old; the same age as her mother when she had died.

The previous year, Patrick Bronte had given his daughter a little bundle of letters. They had been written by her mother Maria to Patrick and it was the first time he had shown them to anyone. She was very touched by these words from a mother she had barely known.

In June of 1855, following Charlotte's death, Patrick Bronte wrote to Elizabeth Gaskell asking her to write Charlotte's biography.

THE BRONTE SISTERS AND THEIR BOOKS

Patrick Bronte had a huge influence on the development of his childrens' literary development and the influence of their home environment was very important in the writings of the three Bronte Sisters, particularly Emily. Her book 'Wuthering Heights' emerges out of the landscape of Haworth, but their novels were also based on other places and events which they had experienced. Charlotte in particular liked to describe people she knew.

Emily used some of the characters and buildings of Southowram where she had briefly worked as a governess. Anne's novels 'Agnes Grey' (1846) and 'The Tenant of Wildfell Hall' described her experiences as a governess.

The first part of Agnes Grey is based on her life in Mirfield where she was governess at Blake Hall. And where she found it impossible to control the children she was teaching.

Charlotte's experiences of life in Brussels helped shape 'The Professor' (1846) and 'Villette' (1853).

But 'Jane Eyre' (1847) and 'Shirley' (1849) had a lot of the Spen Valley in them; both people and places.

Charlotte set her book 'Shirley' in 1811-1812 in the Spen Valley at the time of the Luddites' activities.

The hero was *Robert Moore* (William Cartwright). Charlotte had a problem here because he had to be cast as an authoritarian figure given her own social background, but like her father she had obvious sympathies with the working classes and so she turned him into a man with an eye for progress while he made sure that the unemployed families got food. She shows how the millowners were struggling too in wartime Britain.

She uses Yorkshire dialect to bring her characters to life and real life people to fill her pages. She pokes gentle fun at the three curates of Dewsbury, Birstall and Hartshead, who are only interested in good food, wine and pretty young women. Only the curate of Hartshead was a *'worthwhile fellow,'* (her father?).

She is even more hilarious when describing the warlike *Rev. Helstone* (The Rev. Hammond Roberson) and the way in which he was oblivious to suffering, even that of his dying wife!

She describes the Whitsuntide processions when 12,000 sunday school children from three parishes combined on Briarfield Church (Birstall) for a party of tea and currant buns.

One family she describes in her book is the *Yorke* family (the Taylors).

She admires *Mr. Yorke* for his educated ways, 'A man of remarkable intelligence and strong prejudices all running in favour of Republicanism and Dissent. No other county but Yorkshire could have produced such a man.'

She also used Joshua Taylor as the template of a character in 'The Professor.' She paints a much less pleasant character when she describes *Mrs. Yorke* and her lack of control over her mutinous children. She hints at the future life of *Rose Yorke* (Mary) who talks about her plans to travel the world so as not to become an old maid.

Red House is very recognisable, as is Oakwell Hall which becomes *Fieldhead,* the home of *Shirley Keeldar* where the heroine, *Caroline*, has afternoon tea on the lawn and spends quiet evenings by the fireside in the parlour. *Shirley* is modelled on her sister Emily and *Caroline* on her friend Ellen Nussey.

She says of Fieldhead, 'It stands in a rough looking pasture field a quarter mile from the high road along which you see at meal times strings of mill hands blue with woollen dye. And she describes; The high gable then a long front then a gable; then a thick lofty chimney.'

Even Keeper, Emily Bronte's beloved dog, is portrayed as *Shirley's* faithful friend!

The attack on Rawfolds Mill by the Luddites is central to the plot, being the moment when economic hardship suffered by the workers and their attempts to resist the millowners reached breaking point. It is a story full of drama and accurately describes the night of April 11th 1812 and the relentless pursuit of the Luddites by the authorities. Charlotte researched her story thoroughly from the pages of the Leeds Mercury.

When her book was published there was a lot of interest in the Spen Valley as people speculated as to which characters were drawn from life. Mrs. Taylor was particularly put out by her portrayal.

Goodness knows what the Rev. Hammond Roberson thought of his character! Mary Taylor was very homesick when she read the book in Wellington, New Zealand. She recognised her childhood home and lots of old friends.

The Brontes belong to the Spen Valley as much as to Haworth and in 'Shirley,' the story of local families and the drama of the Luddite attack merge together.

Charlotte Bronte's connections with the Taylor family enabled her to describe the Spen Valley as it was; particularly its inhabitants' well deserved reputation for independent speech and action.

Joshua Taylor was important in his own right as a representative of the middle classes who helped the fortunes of England during the Industrial Revolution.

He was equally important for giving hospitality to a shy vicar's daughter from Haworth.

CHAPTER 9: EDUCATION AND RELIGION IN THE 19th CENTURY

EDUCATION

The Bronte Sisters were engaged in the education of the children of the wealthy middle classes. So what about the rest? The only available statistical yardstick of educational standards in the 18th Century and the early part of the 19th Century is the number of brides and grooms who were unable to sign their names on their marriage certificates. And this shows that in fact, much of the population was illiterate.

Some working class children attended a dame school or a charity school but neither provided a decent education. There was a dame school near Hartshead Church where Nanny Woods taught boys and girls in her little school on Ladywell Lane. This building still exists. You can clearly see Nancy (Nanny) Woods cottage attached to the boys school and the girls school. Hammond Robertson taught boys in his home, Healds House.

Nanny Woods Dame School, Hartshead

In 1808, some townsfolk in Heckmondwike opened a charity school. Benjamin Firth opened a school for boys at Hartshead Moor known as the Manor House Academy (now a Care Home). But these apart, there were virtually no schools for the growing population.

Sunday Schools

This is why Sunday Schools filled such a gap and assumed so much importance. It has, however been suggested that the real motive behind sunday schools was a middle class plot to improve good behaviour in potentially dangerous concentrations of working class communities. The middle classes wanted to keep the workers in their place! These were after all dangerous times.

Possibly this was one of the Reverend Hammond Roberson's considerations, given his views about the Luddites and other working class grievances. Certainly one clergyman from Leeds claimed that teaching methods in the sunday schools, *'Inculcates submission to authority.'*

Whatever the motives behind them, sunday schools provided the only chance of even the most basic education. They taught both reading and writing as well as the scriptures.

Day Schools

From the early 1830's, the combination of legal restrictions on child employment, a rise in working class income and a better provision of day schools meant that the sunday schools ceased to be the main providers of education. The motives behind the middle class promoters of Day Schools were complex. There was the obvious need to educate the younger generation for the sake of the future prosperity of the country as a whole. It was how this education was organised which was the problem.

In this part of the country as elsewhere, the issue was; how were the new schools to teach about religion?

A bitter feud broke out between the Anglicans and the Nonconformist groups about this very point. The Anglican church wanted to provide National Schools with the aid of local subscriptions and grants from the National Society and the Government. Their aim was to stamp out Nonconformism. This led to the Nonconformists building their own day schools, British Schools, but they had far more difficulty finding the funds. They were mainly funded by the British and Foreign Society.

Both provided religious as well as other teaching for poorer children. And both used the Monitorial System where pupil teachers were appointed at the age of 13 to teach smaller groups. In the Spen Valley there were already some of these schools. In 1818, the first National School in the country was built by the Reverend Hammond Roberson at Hightown and pupils were transferred from the small charity school (now a cottage) behind the Town Hall, across Halifax Road to this Anglican school which can still be seen today. It is now made up of apartments. A second National School was built in Oakenshaw in 1822.

National School, Liversedge

In 1834, a British School was built in Cleckheaton, on the site of the present Town Hall, for the Nonconformists. Most of the pupils were factory children.

Only the schoolmaster's house remains (to the left of the Town Hall) but this gives an idea as to the style of the original school building.

St John's Church in Cleckheaton built a National School on Church Street nearby the church, for children of its own parishioners. The stone inscription for this school lies just inside the church-gate. (The school itself is no longer in existence).

Another National School was erected at Scholes in 1837. As late as 1874, the Church of England was building schools like the National School at Hill Top, Gomersal, built in an ecclesiastical style.

Board Schools

Eventually, the 1870 Forster Education Act, made education compulsory from the ages of five to twelve.

This required the building of new schools to cope with the demand. So local groups known as Boards were established to build these brand new schools with money from the rates.

They were to teach the three 'R's; Reading, Writing and Arithmetic and were to enforce strict discipline.

The first Board School in Liversedge was built at Littletown in 1878 for 540 children. There followed one at Hightown, also in 1878, for 450 children; Norristhorpe had 380 children, Roberttown 236 and Millbridge 206.

All the rest of the settlements in the Spen Valley got their own Board Schools after the 1870's. But children could still work part time in the mills and pits.

Littletown Board School

The Education Act of 1880 raised the school leaving age to 13, putting further pressure on the schools.

Attendance at school was now mandatory and children were not supposed to be in part time work. This was the first attempt ever to separate the world of childhood from the world of work.

The School Boards were still elected locally and these elections were fiercely fought between church and chapel.

The 1902 Balfour Education Act ended all this by entrusting education to the County Councils and starting a separate stage of study; the Secondary School. Elementary and Secondary Education was to become the responsibility of local government. Existing Board Schools became Council Schools.

The Mechanics' Institute Movement

The movement towards education did not end with providing schools for children. There was also a movement for educating working men. This gave rise to the Mechanics' Institute Movement which began in London in 1824 and spread quickly after that time. These establishments were distrusted by many in the Church of England who thought they bred political radicalism! Mechanic's Institutes provided libraries and lecture halls and gave valuable opportunities for self-education. They were popular in Yorkshire after the late 1840's.

Local examples of these were the Cleckheaton Mechanics Institute (1837), Heckmondwike Mechanics Institute (1841), Birkenshaw Mechanics' Institute (1848) and Gomersal Mechanics' Institute (1852). They were built by public subscription and filled a useful gap before higher education was introduced. Many were the fore-runners of technical colleges. Women from the working classes were usually denied further education. Most women went into the mills or domestic service and started their families which could be as many as ten children.

Mechanics Institute, Gomersal

Secondary Education

This was encouraged from about 1895 for both boys and girls. Heckmondwike paved the way for secondary education and opened its new Secondary Board School for 900 pupils in 1898. As well as academic tuition, the curriculum included technical and commercial training. Many local people and firms contributed to the building. Heckmondwike thought that this school would be sufficient for the whole valley as it incorporated several local schools, but some thought differently. They were John Mowat, George Whitley, Walter Wadsworth, Reginald Gryllis and Will Clough.

Cleckheaton was not to be outclassed! After 1902 (and the Balfour Act) the Cleckheaton Urban District Council was prepared to build the school without asking for contributions from the County Council (the authority then responsible for higher education). The new school, Whitcliffe Mount, was built on a former football ground in 1910 for 300 pupils. It was Cleckheaton's Secondary and Technical School.

Whitcliffe Mount Secondary School, Cleckheaton

By the end of the century, education had developed to some degree but there were many children still unable to use their education to make any real difference to their lives.

Too many children still spent half the day working in the factories or farms. The Half Time system should have ended with the next education act, the 1918 Education Act, when the school leaving age was raised to 14, but it was not until the early 1920's that it finally disappeared from the valley.

RELIGION

The Spen Valley continued to develop as one of the strongest areas of dissent in the whole country. Many fine buildings appeared; many of which survive to this day.

Frank Peel called the area the 'Metropolis of Dissent.' He said that there was nowhere else in England where Nonconformism had taken such a hold.

Chapel Building

The evangelical revival led by John Wesley, the founder of Methodism, had attracted the people of the Spen Valley.

John Wesley had kept close links with the Church of England but after his death in 1797, Methodists became split into diverse groups, some of them fairly extreme in outlook and doctrine.

Independents, later known as the Congregationalists, were popular in this area. They drew people into the chapels in ever increasing numbers.

This became a century of chapel-building on an epic scale. There were no fewer than eleven chapels built in Cleckheaton (which included Scholes and Oakenshaw).

The first Methodist Chapel in Cleckheaton was Marsh Chapel built in 1811. As Methodism flourished, the Congregationalists began re-building existing chapels into bigger and more imposing ones. These were consciously designed to look different from Anglican churches. In fact some of them looked more like town halls.

An example of this is Providence Place Congregational Chapel in Cleckheaton, built between 1857 and 1859,

It has an arcaded façade with corinthian columns and a flight of steps leading up to it. The effect was very grand.

It seated 1,550 people and underneath the main building were rooms for the all important sunday school. There were 712 scholars and 161 teachers in the 1860's.

Providence Place Chapel, Cleckheaton

The Central Chapel, also in Cleckheaton, built in 1879, was even bigger! It became known as the Cathedral of Free Methodism because of its immense size.

It belonged to the United Methodist Free Church. Its giant portico was flanked by two decorated domed towers and it seated no fewer than 1,764 people. It had a separate sunday school building. An eighty-strong group of people was needed to help the minister with his pastoral work! This chapel stood on the site of the present Post Office and it overlooked the Green.

There was another huge Wesleyan Methodist Church in Whitcliffe Road in Cleckheaton. This one had room for 1,000 people and its sunday school, together with twelve other rooms, lay below the main chapel. Only the name Wesley Street reminds us of this fine building.

The Upper Independent Chapel on High Street Heckmondwike was opened in 1890 but was the fourth on the site. Each re-building was in response to the needs of the growing congregation. This too has an imposing façade with a portico and corinthian columns. It had seating for 1,300 people and was built partly by contributions from the Firth's carpet manufacturing dynasty. The sunday school was built to the side.

The Congregational Church at Norristhorpe was built in 1874 as an offshoot of an earlier version of this chapel.

Grove Congregational Chapel in Gomersal was built in 1825 on land gifted by James Burnley, who was a leading Congregationalist. He paid for some of the building costs too. He had done well out of the Napoleonic Wars and some of his profits went into this chapel.

John Taylor was an admirer of John Wesley who visited Red House several times. But Taylor also enjoyed the sermons of more radical preachers and he built his own chapel, the Red Brick Chapel in Gomersal for these Methodist rebels.

Perhaps the most beautiful chapel in Gomersal is the Wesleyan Methodist Chapel built in 1827 with its unusual curved front. Like most chapels it had an upper and lower gallery to accommodate large congregations. It became affectionately known as the Pork Pie Chapel.

Wesleyan Methodist Chapel, Gomersal

In 1839, the Wesleyan Chapel in Roberttown was erected, in the great centenary year of the Wesleyan Movement.

Many of these chapels are no longer in use or have been turned into homes, shops or restaurants. The Upper Independent Chapel in Heckmondwike has been converted into flats and Providence Place Congregational Chapel in Cleckheaton, closed as a place of worship in 1992, has become an Indian Restaurant. The biggest in the world! This is all to the good because these important buildings are being preserved. Some, unfortunately, have disappeared altogether. An example of the latter is St John's Methodist Church in Hightown.

St John's Methodist Church, Hightown

When Wesley visited the area, he often stayed with Thomas Wright of Lower Blacup Farm.

Wright was a great believer and he helped build the Theyked or thatched chapel in Hightown. This was replaced in 1828 by a large imposing building, St John's Methodist Church, opposite Aquila Way, on Halifax Road. Its huge sunday school building was a little further on, opposite Hightown Board School.

In 1978 the 150th anniversary souvenier booklet describes this church in some detail and the way its activities embraced all aspects of social life. It is worth mentioning some of these to gain an insight into the true importance of 'chapel' in this period.

There was a flourishing cricket club with a pitch and pavilion off Miry Lane and there were tennis courts too. There was an impressive history of choral traditions with concerts featuring the works of Bach, Handel, Haydn and Mozart all of which attracted considerable audiences.

The Cleckheaton Guardian notes on 11th November 1887, *'The first in a series of popular concerts, pre-ceded by a Public Tea took place on Saturday last in Hightown Sunday School. There was a full band and a chorus of 60 performers.'*

There were women's sewing meetings, garments being made for the annual Sale of Work, a library and reading room. There were dramatic groups; the sunday school teachers and youth leaders putting on plays to mark the different anniversaries of the church year. There was a Wesley Guild which organised professional outside speakers and visits.

A Bronte exhibition was permanently available for visiting coach parties to the Spen Valley; many of them using the chapel buildings for lectures and refreshments.

Then there were the harvest festival celebrations and Christmas carol singing expeditions and a rendering of the Messiah in the church. For young people there were many group activities, including conservation work. They too had visiting speakers, including on one occasion the missionary Gladys Aylward! There were fancy dress parades and sports days and lots of other activities.

Sunday school, however, remained a valuable part of the Church and the Sunday School Prize Giving was one of the most important events of the year with a big tea party and concert to follow. Many people kept their sunday school prizes and certificates of attendance all their lives along with their most treasured possessions and these are often discovered by people today who are tracing their family trees.

So the social interaction at all these many places of worship with their weekly meetings and annual bazzars and charabanc trips was a crucially important part of life. Most young people met their spouses at Chapel. Families knew each other more intimately. Communities were bound together by the strong ties of chapel- going.

The Whitsuntide Walks led by brass bands took the chapels to the streets in a glorious day of hymn singing often followed by a sports day and one of their famous teas.

THE QUAKERS

The Society of Friends continued to flourish. The leading role in their story was taken up by the Crosland family of Scholes, so the focus shifted from Hightown and the Greene Family to the nearby village of Scholes and the Croslands who lived at Oldfield-nook.

By the 19th Century, the Crosland family had taken the lead in organising the social and religious activities of the village, at first from the village hall called the Victoria Institute which they built on their land. This was a place of worship, a library and a centre for social activities.

Then in 1888, James Crosland donated land next to his home for a Meeting House and burial ground and this beautiful building survives today. The church continued to flourish with reading groups, sewing groups, Bring and Buy sales, visiting speakers and all the activities which brought a lively social focus to the village.

Friends Meeting House, Scholes

THE MORAVIANS

The Moravians continued to worship in Little Gomersal and in 1870, a second church was built. A Moravian Church was also built in Heckmondwike in 1872 and also in Lower Wyke.

So while there were differences in style between the Nonconformist groups, they all flourished in the 19th Century providing a substantial part of the fabric of social life. There were strict rules on drinking and gambling and a strong ethos on family values.

THE ANGLICAN CHURCH

And what about the Church of England?

The task facing the Anglican vicars was that in this age of rapid social and industrial change, their parishes were just too big to cope.

There had been no new churches built since the Middle Ages. Three churches still served the growing population of the Spen Valley; at Birstall, Whitechapel and Hartshead.

This was all about to be changed by the efforts of one man, the Rev. Hammond Roberson.

THE REVEREND HAMMOND ROBERSON

He has already emerged in our story as an opponent of the Luddites, as an advocate of education and an innovator in local government.

But it was his efforts in re-establishing the Church of England in the Spen Valley and indeed a wider area beyond the Valley, that will be his lasting epitaph.

Roberson had been vicar of Dewsbury and after that Hartshead. He then bought a site on the old Hustings Knoll in Liversedge, where he built a church out of his own money.

At the laying of the foundation stone, in 1812, soldiers had to be in attendance to provide protection if necessary because of the Luddite activities.

He stipulated that all the gravestones in his new churchyard were to be uniform in size. The building was completed in 1816 and was consecrated as the Parish Church of Liversedge.

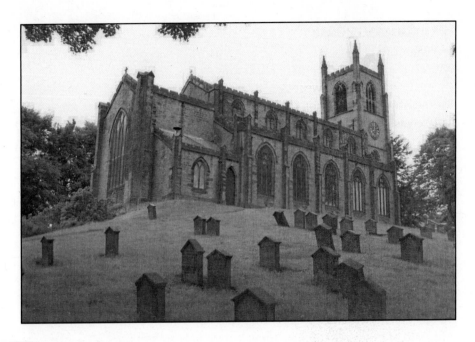

Parish Church of Liversedge

He then went on to make full use of a financial bonanza that became available. In 1818, Parliament voted £1 million towards the building of new churches. Hammond Roberson used his influence to get £5,000 from this Million Fund to build more churches.

St James' in Heckmondwike and St John's in Cleckheaton were built by 1832. The land for St John's became available from the land enclosures.

The Beaumont Family of Bretton Hall bought about 200 acres of land in Cleckheaton when the common fields were enclosed in 1795, but in 1829 they sold off this land so some of it was made available for the purpose of building a church. Cleckheaton got its first Parish Church, St. John's.

Parliament made a further grant and there followed a spate of church building at Roberttown and Birkenshaw, Hightown and Dewsbury Moor.

By 1851, St Mary's was built in Gomersal and St Luke's in Moorbottom, Cleckheaton.

The last two churches were St Philip's and St James' in Scholes which was consecrated by the Bishop of Ripon in 1877 and St Andrew's in Oakenshaw which was completed in 1889.

St. Barnabas Church, Hightown

New vicarages were built to house the vicars of these churches and indeed the old, for example, Sir George Armytage donated land for the building of a vicarage for Hartshead Church in 1872.

This large house stands at the corner of Freak Field Lane and Church Lane on the edge of the Armytage Estate. Its unusual feature is an incomplete set of small gable windows in the shape of a diamond, a spade and a club.

Interesting choice for the home of a vicar!

The three original churches, Whitechapel, Hartshead and Birstall all underwent re-building. The parish of Hartshead-cum-Clifton was split in two by the building of St John's Church in Clifton in 1860. The Clifton graves in Hartshead churchyard are mainly from the period before 1860.

All the Anglican churches flourished but the strength of Nonconformity; politically, socially and numerically always posed problems for the Church of England during the 19th Century.

So, despite his authoritarian ways and his oppostition to radical elements in the local population, Roberson accomplished a great deal.

He breathed new life into the Anglican Church and he was dedicated to the job of educating the young, He really was one of the key characters of the Spen Valley in the 19th Century.

The highlight of the year for Anglicans as with chapel go-ers, was the Whit-Monday Procession when the congregations paraded the streets, dressed in their best clothes and took part in open air services with lots of hymn singing along the way. In Cleckheaton for example there would be around ten sunday school parades followed by a tea and bun 'tuck-in' and sports in various fields around the town.

Churches and chapels did wield a huge influence in education and social welfare. Sunday schools still provided some education for the poor. The pastoral work of clergyman and minister increased as efforts were made to improve social conditions.

There was above all a role of trying to improve the morals of a society badly shaken by the effects of the Industrial Revolution.

Most of those who held important political, commercial or social positions in town would have gone to church or chapel.

Indeed some of them helped to build them!

CHAPTER 10: THE INDUSTRIAL REVOLUTION

Despite the unrest of the early years, the 19th Century saw a steady development in industrial activity and by the middle of the the century the sheer variety of types of industry was quite extraordinary.

Many developed out of the existing cottage industries but all were due in a large part to the appearance of shrewd entrepreneurs (as had happened in previous centuries) and more so now because of available raw materials and also ready markets.

Conversely, some of the older entrepreneurs, for example the Taylors of Gomersal, found their fortunes on the wane. Joshua Taylor's financial problems, caused when his private bank collapsed in 1825, left a generation of his family paying off his debts. But usually, the family businesses of the Spen Valley were successful and each generation added to the achievements of the last.

THE TEXTILE INDUSTRY

The emergence of the Spen Valley as a textile region was a gradual development based on what had gone before.

Entrepreneurs like Cartwright of Rawfolds Mill, adopted new machinery as soon as it was invented. Machinery could be powered by water power and by the middle of the century by steam power. Spinning machines and weaving looms were built on a large scale. This meant bigger and bigger mill buildings to house the enormous machines.

THE MILLS

Mills were built from local sandstone quarried near at hand. They evolved from the early square shape to the long, many storied, many windowed edifices that we still see today. They usually had a large gateway leading into the mill yard, paved with setts.

On one side of the yard would be the owner's house (as had always been the case from the 17th Century on) and this in time was vacated for a new house built at a discreet distance, but never very far. The early industrialists were proud of their achievements and liked to have them in full view.

The weaving sheds were usually one-storied with saw-tooth roofs. The chimneys were the symbols of the power house and the mill dam provided water for the various processes of manufacture. The scale of the new industry was breathtaking.

Mills were extremely large buildings and the large sums of money invested in them, plus the fact that machinery could be used continuously, demanded that they were used day and night. This meant that men and women had to work in shifts throughout a twenty-four hour period.

It meant that the landscape was lit up by rows upon rows of factory windows. And it meant streets upon streets of terraced houses were built rapidly on any vacant land nearby the factories so that the workers could get to work quickly and easily. Towns began to advance over the surrounding fields.

MILLOWNERS

Millowners were constantly facing new challenges; installing the latest machinery and overcoming, the best they could, the effects of foreign tariffs and periods of recession and war. The re-opening of export markets following the Napoleonic Wars in 1815 did a great deal of good to the mill owners of the Spen Valley.

An example of such a millowner is George Anderton who founded his business in 1819. He built a woollen textile mill, Victoria Mill, on Bradford Road Cleckheaton, in 1837 and by the middle of the century, this was an extensive site with a three storey mill for carding, one for spinning, several more weaving sheds and a two storey engine house and separate offices.

Six generations of this family continued the business. In the 1840's Anderton built two houses at the junction of Scott Lane and Bradford Road. They were known as Providence Place (the chapel built opposite them took this name). The houses are now named Elm Bank and The Hollies.

George Anderton was one of the stars of the Spen Valley millowners. He was an entrepreneur 'par excellence.' He was a Liberal and a Nonconformist and his highly principled values came to the fore when it came to helping the working classes. He was a pioneer of education and in 1836 was instrumental in getting the British School built in Cleckheaton (on the site which became the Town Hall).

He was a member of the Anti-Corn Law League which was trying to keep food prices low for the working class. He was Spen's very own Railway King often attending the sittings of Parliament to watch over the various Bills put forward by the Lancashire and Yorkshire Railway Company (which was buying up land) so that when the time was ripe he could ensure a railway link could pass through the Spen Valley for the benefit of all the local millowners.

He was a Guardian of the Poor at Staincliffe Workhouse. He formed the new Local Board in Cleckheaton which provided a water and gas supply to the town. He was an inventor, creating one of the first Combing Machines in the woollen industry. And he managed to run a very large mill at the same time!

His son William continued in much the same vein. He helped found the Mechanics Institute in Cleckheaton, was a prime mover in the building of the Providence Place Chapel and he laid the foundation stone for the Town Hall.

Another example of these enterprising families was the Cooke family of Heckmondwike. Their company was founded by William Peabody Cooke in 1795, one of the first to make carpets in Heckmondwike.

But it was his son Samuel who began to specialise in Brussels carpets who really improved the fortunes of his Company.

By 1834, he had an eight horse-power steam engine and employed 27 workpeople spinning yarn. The carpets were still produced on handlooms.

By 1870 however, the carpet business was totally mechanised and Cooke's employed 500 people at their Millbridge works.

Cooke's Mill had three different buildings spanning all the main thoroughfares in the village. They dominated the Millbridge skyline.

Samuel Cooke bought Healds House as his family home, the former home of the Reverend Hammond Roberson.

Millbridge Spinning Company – part of the original Cooke's Mill

Yet another famous firm, Firths, started in 1822 when Edwin Firth built a weaving shed in Heckmondwike. He supplied the yarn for local people to weave on their handlooms. He then bought the cloth and finished it in his own workshop.

His business flourished so he took over Flush Mills, in Heckmondwike, for the manufacture of blankets, the main product of Heckmondwike weavers. He built up an export trade with North America and built himself a fine house, Flush House, across the road from the mill in what is now Firth Park. In the Crimean War, he produced army cloths and blankets for both the British and French armies.

His son, Thomas Freeman Firth, extended the use of steam power and began carpet making at the mill. He became a Baronet. Under his son, Algernon Firth, the 2nd Baronet, business continued to prosper and he built another huge factory at Bailiffe Bridge. This gave rise to the settlement of Bailiffe Bridge. He even set up mills in the United States of America, Firthcliffe (north of New York) and other towns. Firths became one of America's largest carpet producers.

For 150 years, Firths was the biggest mill in Heckmondwike. All the members of the family played a major role in public affairs in the town. Thomas Freeman Firth was a generous supporter of the Upper Independent Chapel and a County Alderman. His son Algernon Firth was a great philanthropist and commissioned the Algernon Firth Institute of Pathology at the Leeds General Infirmary which he opened in 1933. He was also involved in the struggle for getting better housing for the working classes. Fittingly it is his name that graces the new Health Centre in Heckmondwike.

Elymas Wadsworth ran Broomfield Mills at Moorbottom, Cleckheaton. By 1862, he employed over 600 people and he was Cleckheaton's first representative on the County Council in 1889, chairman of the Higher Education Committee and chairman of the committee to build the Town Hall.

William Atkinson owned St Peg's Mill, Cleckheaton. The name St Peg's interestingly comes from Saint Margaret the patron saint of spinning. This was therefore appropriately involved in the Worsted yarn spinning process.

The mill occupied a huge area consisting of a large block of four storey buildings erected in the form of a hollow square. Interior spiral staircases were built in the corners of the building to save space. This proved an advantage as machinery was always packed together too closely.

The Atkinsons lived at first on the mill premises but later moved to nearby Spen House, up Spen Lane. Their mill was the second largest worsted spinners with a work force of 366. The largest was Anderton's with 386 workers.

The most extensive mill development was along the banks of the Spen River. Mills hugged the sides of the Spen River all the way. In Cleckheaton; the Taylor's Hunsworth Mill (woollen) was at the western part of the valley. Charles Hirst's Exchange Mill was nearby. This mill manufactured iron and steel wire and sold its products as far afield as France, Germany and Belgium. Samuel Law's Moorland Mill was the largest carding mill in Cleckheaton. Then came Waterfield Mill (woollen), Anderton's Victoria Mill (worsted), Springfield Mill (carding), Atkinson's St Peg's Mill and Wesley Barraclough's Marsh Mill (woollen flannel))

Continuing down the valley, in Littletown there was Victoria Mill (woollen) and in Millbridge, Wellington Mills (woollen) and Cooke's Spen Valley Works (carpets).

In Heckmondwike there was Firth's Flush Mill (carpets), Fairfax Kelly's Union Mill (woollen), Wesley Barraclough's Providence Mill (woollen), Benjamin Rhodes' Spen Vale Mill (woollen and worsted yarn spinners) and Michael Swallow's Croft Mill which developed into one of the largest industrial undertakings of its kind for the manufacture of carpets and rugs.

Not all mills occupied the valley floor.

There were mills scattered throughout the area, like Thomas Hemingway's Hare Park Mill, Rayner's Mill at the top of Hare Park Lane (on the site of Jackson's cropping shop), Joseph Lister's Clough Mill, John Hemingway's Roberttown Mill and Roe-Head Mill.

Most of these were carding mills but sometimes there was a change of use, for example Hemingway's on Hare Park Lane, built in 1844, started out as a carding mill and then changed to woollen production and after that leather work. There were three Shoddy mills in Heckmondwike and one at White Lee, all away from the valley.

In Gomersal, the Burnleys continued to prosper. William Burnley had started an early factory in 1752 near to his rented home, Pollard Hall. By 1843, Thomas Burnley was rich enough to buy Pollard Hall.

He enlarged his mill, the Cloth Hall Mill (on the site of the short- lived Cloth Hall of the previous century) and re-named it Gomersal Mills. It had four reservoirs and a dye house. He specialised in wool combing, spinning and dyeing and he produced both weaving and hosiery yarns.

He built up the largest textile business in the village and turned Pollard House into the grandest Victorian mansion in Gomersal. The village of Gomersal began to grow as industry developed.

There was another type of textile mill in Gomersal by 1825. This was a small Silk mill at the bottom of Moor Lane. This is where hand loom silk weaving was carried out by the Porritt family. This was destined to remain a small operation though because of its lack of water power for harnessing machinery.

By 1889, the Trades Directory for Gomersal mentions an Arthur Porritt as the village's only silk manufacturer.

It is still possible to visit this three storey building and stand in the well lit upper storey where the silk looms were housed.

The Old Silk Mill, Moor Lane, Gomersal

In Birkenshaw, the advent of industry brought about a completely new settlement. We last mentioned Birkenshaw as a small settlement on the lower slopes of a ridge of land about a mile away from Gomersal and in the area we now call Birkenshaw Bottoms. The area occupied by the present day village would have been very unsuitable for a settlement in those far off days when the Anglo-Saxon invaders were looking for places to live. It is on a narrow steep slope of very high ground with little protection from the prevailing winds.

But at the end of the 18th Century, John Emmet built a furnace for iron smelting. The Emmet family were responsible for the growth of a new village because they bought up more and more land as their industry grew.

The iron works stretched down to the present Blue Hills Farm which takes its name from the blue-coloured shale taken from the ironworks. There is still a Furnace Lane and Emmet Hill where the family home was built.

Houses were also built for the workforce as the population grew. The iron industry was however very short-lived. When the ironworks closed after the Napoleonic Wars, coalmining and textiles filled the gap in the employment prospects for the villagers of Birkenshaw.

The Oddy family was the main textile firm at the top end of the village. James Oddy and his sons built several small mills and in 1854 the much larger Moorland Mills. The family home was Lapwater Hall and later two more family homes were built, Moorland Hall and Moorville Hall. They also built housing for their workers around Moorlands Square and Southfield Terrace. The family were staunch Methodists and philanthropists. They built Westgate Hill Wesleyan Methodist Church and East Bierley Memorial Hall.

A second family, the Ackroyds, set up as worsted spinners and manufacturers at the lower part of the village. They lived in Oakroyd Hall, now the Fire Service Headquarters. They were staunch Anglicans and supported the newly formed parish. Indeed they donated the land on which the parish church of St Paul's, one of the Million Act Churches, was built. They also opened a colliery and a saw mill so these industries gave further impetus to the growth of Birkenshaw.

Oakenshaw, like Birkenshaw, was completely changed by industrial development. For centuries, Oakenshaw was a tiny agricultural hamlet with farms passed down through generations of the same families. In the 17th and 18th Centuries there were a few cloth workers but in 1848, the railway from Mirfield to Low Moor passed through Oakenshaw and this changed the hamlet for ever. A huge worsted mill was erected and rows of workers cottages. The population increased and a Wesleyan Chapel was built in 1874 and a church, St Andrew's, in 1889. A new road linking Cleckheaton to Low Moor opened up the village even further.

THE MILL WORKERS

The most dramatic effect of the Industrial Revolution was the way in which the lives of ordinary people were changed for ever.

Before the 1850's, work involved farming and cloth production to fit in with the hours of daylight, farming jobs etc. Much of the spring and summer would be spent in farming and in the winter months, families would spend time indoors producing cloth. The whole family shared the jobs involved in both. There were no set hours and discipline was sorted out within the family. There was indeed no separate period of childhood. Children worked alongside their parents and grandparents doing any jobs they were capable of.

When families moved into the mills to work, they were separated according to their age and sex; different jobs for men, women and children. They had to work by the clock. They had strict times for breakfast and dinner. And they were subjected to rules and regulations and fined for any misdemeanours, especially for being late. Millowners were strict disciplinarians but equally they became father figures in their world, that of the mill.

Workers were summoned to work by a buzzer or a whistle. Both men and women wore clogs. Women wore woollen shawls over their dresses. They all carried their meals in a handkerchief or a basket. This meant the women had to make bread and dripping sandwiches for the entire family before work each day. Mostly food was eaten at the loom gate or on the floor leaning against the spinning mules. There was usually a tank of hot water heated by the steam from the engine, where they could mash tea in pint pots.

The deafening noise of machinery forced them to lip read and often caused hearing problems. Some suffered from deformities in the spine from their work, bending over the machines. There was the problem of breathing in dust from the fibres, particularly in the shoddy trade.

Accidents were common (as there were no guards on the machinery) especially among children who were often employed as Pieceners, picking up the loose threads underneath the moving machinery.

At first mills were run on 12 hour shifts and children as young as five or six years of age worked from 6 o'clock in the morning until 6 o'clock at night.

Leeds-born Richard Oastler was one of the main champions of the mill workers and largely because of his efforts, the Ten Hour Bill, was passed by Parliament which stipulated that no-one could work longer than ten hours and children under nine were prevented from working in the mills at all. Much later came legislation regarding the safety of machinery.

The mill buildings themselves were not always safe. In 1892 one of the Spen Valley's greatest tragedies happened when the 150ft chimney at Marsh Mills in Cleckheaton collapsed, killing fifteen people. The chimney weighed 500 tons and it crashed through the roof of the four storey building trapping workers under the rubble.

OTHER INDUSTRIES

There were many more industries which were ancillary to the woollen industry.

There were plenty of dye works dying the yarn for the woollen mills and carpet mills, like the Victoria Dyeworks at Hightown, and also chemical works like the Spen Valley Chemical Works on Bradford Road and the Flatt Lane Chemical works on Whitechapel Lane in Cleckheaton. There were two chemical works in Heckmondwike.

There were several wool and waste merchants (Shoddy) in the area. Their mills mixed reprocessed wool with new wool to produce Mungo and Shoddy for cheap but high quality blankets. Heckmondwike had over a dozen wool and waste merchants, like Darnbrook and Sons on Croft Lane.

Another associated trade was Fellmongering which involved the removal of the wool from the sheepskins. One of the fellmongers of the region was Arthur Lambert at his Union Mills on Beck Lane Heckmondwike.

Hearl Heaton and Sons Ltd made accessories for the textile trade at their Crown Works on Station Road, Liversedge. Accessories like grinding frames, bobbins and loom spindles. This firm began as far back as 1809.

Many people were involved in the spin-off from textiles including actual machine manufacture. There were a number of engineering firms which grew up producing textile machinery, like Blackburn's of Toft's Mill Cleckheaton. Machine making became an important industry in Cleckheaton from the 1830's, the decade in which the town grew rapidly.

But two of the biggest of the ancillary businesses were the carding business and its twin, the wire-working industry. Both of these industries began to flourish and particularly in Cleckheaton.

Card making was a very old industry. For centuries it had been carried out by hand. The actual word 'card' comes from the Latin Cardus which means Thistle. Historically it was the head of the dried thistle which was used for straightening the fibres of wool ready for the spinning process.

We have already seen that there was a trade in Hand Cards which were pieces of leather punched with iron wire staples, made by women and children in the home. This domestic industry had been associated with Scholes and Cleckheaton since the 17th Century.

By 1800, hand carding was being replaced by machinery. The Bendigo Machine and the Stang Machine replaced hand carding. The hand carders became employees operating machines.

Cleckheaton and the nearby village of Scholes remained the main centres for the industry, but as already mentioned, there were several other carding mills scattered throughout the Spen Valley region.

As far back as 1717, Robert Crosland, the Quaker, had started his business at Oldfieldnook in Scholes and this grew in the 19th Century. The Croslands were at the forefront of the new technology in the 1830's by mechanising card setting. They built a mill near to their home and introduced steam power and their own wire-drawing machinery in the 1840's.

Samuel Law started his card making business among the little workshops clustered along Westgate at the turn of the century. By 1864 he had built the large Moorland Mill for his thriving business.

Henry Birkby ran the Pyenot Hall Works at Cleckheaton and he lived at nearby Pyenot Hall, an 18th Century house in large grounds (on the site of the old Pyenot home of the Lords of Heckmondwike and Heaton). After the Birkbys the Hall was occupied by the Goldthorpes and then the Smiths, all of whom ran the Pyenot Hall Works, which by the 1890's was one of the most important wire producing factories in Cleckheaton.

Wire was needed for the teeth on the cards. There were more than a dozen factories involved in this. Cleckheaton could boast it was the Cardmaking Capital of the World!

Edward Brook's Tannery in Cleckheaton, founded back in 1712, was still being run by the family and the business had extended to cover a large site on Valley Road. Brook's supplied leather to cardmakers like Samuel Law and they also made belting to drive machinery in the mills. Tanneries became much larger enterprises than they had been a hundred years before.

John and Edwin Lawford were curriers and leather merchants at their massive Spen Valley Leather Works in Liversedge, which was between Station Road (now Halifax Road) and Ashton Clough Road.

There was, therefore, a variety of industries flourishing in the area, some of them spawned by the needs of the textile mills; others by the demands of a growing population.

A boot and shoe manufacturers was set up by the Wholesale Cooperative Society in Heckmondwike in 1880.

It employed over 400 people and was known locally as the Goliath Boot and Shoe Factory. It occupied a huge site on Brunswick Street in Heckmondwike.

Co-op Boot and Shoe Company, Heckmondwike

Nearby a typical row of terrace houses was built for the workers. It specialised in the manufacture of hard wearing boots for the workers in the mills and the coalmines. Between six and eight thousand pairs of boots were produced each week. Boots were also made for farmers, navvies, quarrymen, police and firemen.

The Cooperative Movement was a direct result of the poverty experienced by working class people. Tradesmen banded together to open their own stores and factories for the benefit of the workers themselves and not the middle classes. Factories like Goliath were a good example of the cooperative ethos because its employees were well looked after; for example, the eight hour working day was introduced as well as a convalescence home built for sick workers.

So the stone built mills with their rows upon rows of terraced houses, began to dominate the landscape. Factory building was made possible by more and more land becoming available because of the enclosures of fields and village greens; the last ones being in Cleckheaton and Scholes.

But none of this would have happened without the wealthy entrepreneurs who were willing and inventive enough to take risks and embark on large enterprises. These men still built their grand family homes adjacent to their workplace, just as in previous centuries when the workshop occupied the garden of the main house.

THE COAL AND IRON INDUSTRY

There was another, profoundly important reason why industry developed on such a large scale in the Spen Valley. That was the availability of coal and iron.

Coal mining was not new in the valley. The first coalpits we hear of, in the 14th Century, were shallow pits worked by a few men who were also farmers. Sir Philip Carey had become very interested in land rich in coal deposits in Elizabethan times.

Three hundred years later, it became one of the main industries of the area with several hundred men (women and children too before 1842) employed in dangerous and unhealthy conditions in the many pits, some of the largest, at Gomersal, and Stanley Pits in Liversedge, being very deep.

The escarpments around the Spen Valley produced two famous coal seams; the Better Bed and the Black Bed.

This was the coal destined to power the steam engines of Spen's mills. But the escarpments contributed something more than coal. Immediately above the Black Bed coal seams there were found shales containing layers of ironstone. This ironstone was of exceptional purity and especially good for drawing into the fine wire used by the card manufacturers.

The LOW MOOR COMPANY

The Low Moor Company bought large tracts of this mineral wealth and by 1863, they employed 3,600 men.

The employees were made up of nearly 2,000 miners, 770 forgemen, 420 furnace men, 323 engineers and 94 managers. The Company worked as many as 70 pits during the 19th century and in the year 1885 was the biggest iron producer in the whole of Yorkshire. It covered an area of Low Moor, Bierley, Cleckheaton, Scholes and several nearby hamlets.

The iron ore was a superior quality and the coal was ideal for smelting because it was free from impurities such as sulphur and phosphorus. This made it the best type of coal to use in both furnace and forge. In fact the excellent quality of the iron was due to the purity of the Better Bed coal.

The Black Bed coal was excellent steam coal for use in the factories.

The Low Moor Company created an enormous iron founding and engineering complex producing steam engines and armaments and castings. There were about 23 pits working in the immediate area, most owned by the Low Moor Company but some were privately owned, for example, the Croslands of Oldfieldnook owned their own.

Nearly all the coal and iron was carried to the furnaces at Low Moor on tramways from various branch lines joining the coal pits.

One of these was from the Three Nuns Pit up to Hartshead, then from Hartshead to Scholes, then Scholes to Wyke and from there by locomotive to Low Moor. Steam winding engines were used to haul the coal up the steep gradients in three successive stages of rope haulage. There was also a narrow gauge line running down to the coal staithes near the canal basin at Brighouse. This was for the coal not required at Low Moor. Ingenious!

Very little remains of the tramway, but earthworks in the region of Clifton as well as the cutting linking the Three Nuns to Hartshead can still be seen.

COALMINES

There were, in addition to the Low Moor collieries, over 50 pits in the area.

In Liversedge these numbered Strawberry Bank at Millbridge, Quaker Lane, Smithy Hill, Stanley Main and Tanhouse Mill among them. In Cleckheaton there was the large Chairbarrows Pit. In Heckmondwike there was Victoria Colliery and Park Farm Colliery and there was a large coal pit at White Lee and at Gomersal.

By the 19th Century, manorial control of Gomersal, centering on Oakwell, had ceased. This enabled the sinking of deep mines at Oakwell. The Ackroyds of Birkenshaw opened a colliery in Birkenshaw linked to this. Kingsley Drive in Birkenshaw was formerly known as Pit Lane.

THE COLLIERS

They would rise at 5.30am and set off walking to the pit head at 6am, armed with their bread and dripping and a pint of cold tea. They wore clogs on their feet and carried their safety lamps. After descending the mine shaft, they trammed their way on a flat board mounted on four wheels, on underground rails, until they came to the gate where they were working. They worked at the seams with 4lb picks and two types of shovel; a round Muck shovel and a square Filling shovel.

They worked in very low tunnels helped by Hurriers, boys over the age of 13 (supposedly) who pushed the tubs of coal from the coal face. The hurriers graduated to colliers when they reached the age of 21.

The collier was paid for the amount of coal he produced. A good collier could get out 2 tons a day. A Weigh-man (for the company) and Check-Weighman (for the colliers) sat in the office at the pit head and weighed the coal.

Working conditions were appalling, partly due to the coal seams often being no more than three feet high and also because there was a total disregard for the dangers of mining in these conditions, such as flooding, roof collapse and explosions. There was the added danger of contracting mining-related diseases.

The coal and dirt that came out of the coal mines had to be separated by washing. The dirt was dumped in spoil heaps which covered all the surrounding fields.

On the actual site of the coal mine there was a large collection of mine buildings.

The Winding Engine which operated the mine shafts was the main feature of the site. There were other engine houses, a building for the powder magazines, washers, and dirt hoppers. Then there was the canteen, baths, weigh office, other offices, the lamp room and work shops. These all took up a considerable area.

At Gomersal Pit they covered the area that today is occupied by Oakwell Hall country park and its car park.

So this industry, no less than the textile industry changed the landscape. The spoil heaps and winding gear, the mineral railways and mining cottages became features of the Spen Valley. Air pollution was now a fact of life.

This was described by Charlotte Bronte in 'Shirley' when she talks about a pitch black night only illuminated by the, *'Furnaces of Stilbro (Low Moor) throwing a tremulous lurid shimmer on the horizon.'*

And she describes the mill chimneys of the Spen Valley, *'Sulphur - puff from the soot thick columns of smoke rushing sable from the gaunt mill chimneys.'*

CHANGES BROUGHT ABOUT BY THE INDUSTRIAL REVOLUTION

SOCIAL LIFE

Social life was dominated by the mill and the pit. A typical working day started at 6am and ended at 5.30pm. There was a half hour for breakfast and half an hour for dinner. The start of each work period was sounded by a 5 minute whistle which reverberated throughout the surrounding area.

Wages were very low and children; both half-timers and those who had left school at thirteen, would bring in urgently needed money. Birth control was either not known or not practised and so families of up to ten children were very common. Women could be bearing children for a period of ten years or more. This was at a terrible cost to their health. Many babies didn't survive infancy. So this precarious start in life plus all the dangers associated with the industries which grew up in the area meant that life expectancy was short.

THE LANDSCAPE

The Industrial Revolution changed forever the landscape of the Spen Valley as it did in many parts of the British Isles.

The introduction of steam power led to an intense concentration of large scale industry for the first time. This required a huge labour force of men women and children. Manufacturers built their mills and factories in the existing towns (which were mainly in valleys).

The workers were housed in streets of terrace houses built hurriedly close by the mills. These were, therefore, on low lying ground which presented drainage problems, and sanitation conditions soon became appalling.

To make matters worse, the houses were often poorly built. There were several reasons for this. There had been a sharp rise in the price of building materials due to the Napoleonic Wars. Interest rates too had increased rapidly and land had become more expensive. So this resulted in a drastic reduction in the size and quality of workers houses in order to achieve an economic rent.

There were also unscrupulous speculators using inferior building materials. And houses were built in long terraces because they used up less land, and back to back terraces used even less land.

Open spaces vanished. Liversedge lost its village green which was near the old Lower Hall on Halifax Road. Cleckheaton Green almost disappeared and only strong local opposition in Heckmondwike helped the Green survive there, albeit much truncated. The new landscape was dramatically different and not in a good way for those who lived there.

TRANSPORT AND COMMUNICATIONS

ROADS

Manufacturers demanded improved communications and the lack of a sizeable river or canal in the Spen Valley was an obvious hindrance.

The railways had not yet been invented so for the first half of the 19th Century, roads had to be sufficient for the ten mile radius involved in trade with the major centres of the West Riding; Bradford, Huddersfield, Wakefield and Leeds.

By now, wheeled traffic had replaced packhorses so this meant improving the turnpike roads of the previous century.

There was also the urgent need to build more turnpike roads.

In 1803 the Millbridge to Cleckheaton road was the first of these, connecting Cleckheaton with Liversedge at last and providing a route through the Spen Valley to Bradford (the present A638). The main importance of Bradford Road was to turn the interest of Spen Valley from Leeds towards Bradford, a change re-inforced later by the coming of the railways.

In 1824 the Holme Lane End and Heckmondwike Turnpike replaced the old hill top road through Gomersal leading to Birkenshaw.

Previous to this the main road had continued down Knowles Hill past The Shoulder of Mutton pub.

In 1825 the Leeds and Whitehall Trust constructed their road from Leeds to Halifax which was 14 miles in length. This completely replaced the old road which had been turnpiked in the previous century (the old Leeds-Elland road which went through Birstall and down Spen Lane through Cleckheaton and over Hartshead Moor).

In 1826, the Dewsbury to Gomersal road was built (the A652 Bradford Road) and in 1834, a turnpike road was built between Leeds and Huddersfield which by-passed Roberttown.

So the first part of the century saw a speculative boom when lots of Trusts were set up. By 1848, Toll Bar Houses had been erected for the keepers of tolls at Spen, White Lee, Hightown, Gomersal, Castle Hill and of course Chain Bar. There were three toll houses on Whitehall Road one of the most important turnpike roads.

The toll bar house at the junction of Huddersfield Road and Roberttown Lane can still be seen. This was built for the Birstall and Huddersfield Turnpike and the windows on every side of the building shows how the toll keeper could have good visibility along both roads.

Toll Bar House, Roberttown

The coaching inns took on a new role as the Royal Mail coaches stopped there; inns such as the Globe Inn at Millbridge which stood on the Leeds-Huddersfield-Manchester highway.

The landlord of The Globe Inn was George Humble, a bit of a local character. Regular coaching services had started back in the 1780's as a direct result of turnpiking and Birstall, Gomersal, Cleckheaton and Millbridge had become important coaching centres.

By the 19th Century, these services had increased and the Royal Mail thundered through Liversedge twice a day. It was painted scarlet and had the Royal Coat of Arms emblazoned on the sides and back. As it swung down the hill towards Millbridge, the guard would blow a loud blast on his horn to warn the postman to catch the postbag.

The main stopping places were The Nag's Head (which became The George in 1840) The Globe Inn, The Yew Tree and The Star Inn.

At The Yew Tree (now Headlands Hall) the well can still be seen from where the water was drawn for the horses.

Yew Tree Inn, Roberttown

Mail coach guards carried blunderbusses for protection. These were made in London for the Royal Mail between 1788 and 1816. They were very effective weapons because they discharged small shot over a wide area at short range. The guard couldn't really miss! After the 1820's, flintlock pistols were used.

Only a couple of minutes were taken to change all four horses at coaching inns and ostlers were penalised for not having fresh horses ready at the correct time. Mail coaches alone were allowed to pass through the toll gates without stopping.

By the 1850's, most of the the toll bar buildings and many of the inns had fallen out of use.

Between 1864 and 1895 all roads were Dis-Turnpiked and put under local government supervision. The roads themselves ceased to be important.

A new form of transport had arrived, the railways.

RAILWAYS

The Spen Valley was seen as an important route way for a railway, which would link the area not just with the West Riding towns, but with the rest of the country. This would allow industry to compete on a wider stage.

George Anderton, the pioneer of the worsted trade, was the prime mover in getting the railway through the valley.

He bought shares in the West Riding Junction Railway Company and became a Director of the Lancashire and Yorkshire Railway and then he bought land from Mirfield all the way to Low Moor! This meant that when the Lancashire and Yorkshire Railway opened in 1848, he was able to run a branch line from Mirfield to Low Moor, which by 1850 was connected to Bradford.

Three stations were built along this line, at Heckmondwike, Liversedge and Cleckheaton. The three towns of the valley were connected and the line was for the use of passengers as well as freight.

The commercial advantages were of huge importance. Raw materials could be brought in for the valley's textile (and other) industries and finished products could be carried to much wider markets.

The social impact was tremendous too. The railway linked individual villages so that they grew and spread outwards blurring the dividing lines between them.

This helped to make towns and villages more united in their customs and traditions. For example the Cleckheaton Holidays were adopted throughout the district. Mills closed down for the same weeks each year.

People travelled a great deal more. They not only travelled outside their villages for the first time but they visited the large towns of West Yorkshire and beyond.

Their diets were improved by the fact that fresh food like fish, fruit and vegetables could be transported quickly. There was now a much bigger variety of food for even the poorest of people.

Newspapers and post could also be carried more easily and this opened up the world outside even further. As education developed and literacy improved, many people could now read newspapers and see what was going on at home and abroad. The isolation of villages and hamlets was ended for ever.

In 1892, the London and North West Railway Company built another line, this time on the eastern side of the valley. This was to link the existing lines to the National Rail network. This provided further stations at Heckmondwike and Cleckheaton and one at Gomersal.

This was the last rail link to be built in West Yorkshire (Spen Station at Cleckheaton was opened in 1900) It was 13.5 miles long and ran from the east of Huddersfield to west Leeds.

The impact of railways on the environment was also far reaching. Ordinance Survey maps of the time show huge swathes of land occupied by railway lines, stations and goods yards, embankments, cuttings and tunnels.

There was some spectacular civil engineering, including rail viaducts in Heckmondwike and a tunnel, 30 feet below Gomersal, which was 890 feet long.

An outstanding Victorian viaduct was built across the River Spen, to give Cleckheaton people (and horse drawn carriages) access between the two stations.

Viaduct, Cleckheaton

The late completion of the railway through Heckmondwike meant that there were great difficulties to overcome because the town was now so built up. The answer was the construction of deep stone-lined cuttings and nine Over Bridges.

The railway stations, very close to the town centres, were handsome buildings with a station master's office, ladies' and gents' waiting rooms and long platforms decorated with canopies. In some places, like Oakenshaw, the railway had transformed a tiny hamlet.

But it was the impact on industry which was all important. Railway Mania in the Spen Valley gave a huge impetus to industry. Textiles, coal, iron and machinery could be readily transported to a much wider market.

CHAPTER 11: IMPROVEMENTS IN PUBLIC HEALTH AND CHANGING TOWNSCAPES

IMPROVEMENTS IN PUBLIC HEALTH

Changes in industry and transport, the Industrial Revolution, changed society too.

By the middle of the century, population growth was phenomenal. Heckmondwike for example had been transformed from a little village into a smoke-filled, crowded industrial town; its population growing from 1,742 in 1801 to 9,459 in 1901. The Parish of Birstall as a whole grew from 13,988 in 1801 to 64,424 in 1901.

At the start of the century, town affairs were conducted, throughout the valley, on an informal basis by elected officials who met in the local inn. This was obviously not enough. These rapidly growing towns were suffering problems that could not be addressed in this way.

For example, the Liversedge Town's Book of 1820 has an entry on September 27th which says, '*At a meeting of the inhabitants of the said township called in the usual manner held this day at the Yew Tree Inn, in Liversedge, for the purpose of choosing a constable and nominate proper persons to serve in the office of Highways for the ensuing year. Resolved that John Dearnley is a proper person for a constable.*'

In a few short years these local groups of '*proper persons*' were out of their depth with the problems that arose from the industrial revolution.

Housing

Families were now living close by the mills and pits and quarries. They lived in rows of terraced houses hurriedly erected to absorb this growing demand. These houses were often shoddily built and poorly ventilated as very often they were back-to-back and one up & one down.

Most had a cellar; a living room about 12 feet by 14 feet, with a staircase in one corner leading to the bedroom, and outside, a shared privy. Several families shared one toilet.

Water Supply and Sewage Disposal

This put enormous pressure on the supply of water and the disposal of sewage.

Water was still supplied by wells, so there was no running water inside the houses or indeed for the outside toilets. Diseases like smallpox, tuberculosis, and scarlet fever spread because of people living in such close proximity, but it was the water-borne diseases of cholera and typhoid which were the most deadly.

Inadequate sewerage and drainage were also major causes of disease. Filthy ashpits (from the coal fires), dry toilets (shared Middens) and piles of refuse in the yards of back-to-back streets, caused obvious health problems. The Spen beck was polluted from industrial processes and sewage alike.

These problems were found right across industrial Britain. Edwin Chadwick MP had highlighted the need for reform, and the Public Health Act of 1848 provided the basis for a new and broader aspect of local government to deal with these issues.

In 1866, the Sanitary Act compelled local authorities to appoint Sanitary Inspectors who were empowered to take action on water, sewage and drainage.

Then in 1871, Local Government Boards were set up to deal with Public Health, just as the School Boards were building new schools. These new Authorities had a major task on their hands. They had to find and supply fresh water for thousands of people. They had to build large sewage and drainage schemes. And they had to find the funding for both.

Unfortunately the three authorities of Heckmondwike, Liversedge and Cleckheaton did not pool their resources. In fact they fell out and bickered between themselves and some even tried to take control over others! In 1864, Heckmondwike and Cleckheaton tried to partition Liversedge between them, and in 1867, Dewsbury tried to incorporate Heckmondwike.

Frank Peel writes at some length about the efforts of individual townspeople. The leading social reformers were those same men who had supported the Chartist movement and the building of schools and chapels. They were often Nonconformists and driven by strong moral principles. In Heckmondwike, he tells us they were, Mr. Joseph Crabtree, Mr. Benjamin Rhodes, Mr. L. Firth and Mr. Hadfield.

They set up an Inquiry and it was found that, *'The population of Heckmondwike has increased from 3,537 in 1841 to 4,540 in 1851 and in addition to 939 dwelling houses there are seven woollen mills, one corn mill, two carpet and coverlet mills, one dye works, four coalmines and a railway. The rate of mortality is high; 26 per 1,000. The water is of poor quality and altogether insufficient for the wants of the inhabitants.'*

The local wells which had once been so plentiful, were no longer sufficient to supply water on such a scale. The result was that Heckmondwike got a Local Board of Health as early as 1853.

Improvements

The new Local Board of Health in Heckmondwike dealt with the water problem by joining with Dewsbury and Batley in the construction of a reservoir at Dunford Bridge, high in the Pennines.

This was a very costly scheme and the representatives of Batley were worried about the costs and about the amount of water supply being insufficient, and they pulled out. Dewsbury and Heckmondwike persevered and got their supplies.

Eighteen miles of brick and iron pipe conduits carried the water which syphoned it into four local reservoirs. The drainage problems were sorted out over the next few years.

Ten years later, Cleckheaton was forced to make similar reforms. Until then the main function of local government in Cleckheaton was to collect the Poor Rates and mend the highways. The social reformers of Cleckheaton who made up the Cleckheaton Local Board of Health, met at The George Hotel on 25th March 1863 and James Anderton was appointed Chairman.

It was decided to apply to Bradford Corporation to see if they would undertake the supply of water. They agreed, but this meant bringing pipes through the Low Moor tunnel, so they needed permission from the Lancashire and Yorkshire Railway Company who were reluctant as they thought water pipes would get damaged from being so close to the rails.

Mr. Anderton intervened and the railway company finally agreed and the water supply system was built and eventually extended to parts of Liversedge.

The Cleckheaton Board had problems too when it came to sewage disposal. They needed to carry a drain through the property of the Cooperative Society, which refused permission. This led to an expensive legal battle, the result of which was that the Local Boards from then on were empowered to have Easement through private property.

The improvements in sanitary conditions in Heckmondwike and Cleckheaton, led Liversedge people to try to get their own Local Board. However, there were many who opposed this, thinking that reforms would be too expensive.

The battle was fought out in the local papers just as today and in January 1872, a public meeting held to try and form such a Board was broken up by opponents.

Frank Peel describes the rioting people marching through the town with a brass band at their head. An excited crowd was present as the meeting opened and the arguments that followed seemed impossible to resolve.

In the end, common sense prevailed and a Local Government Act was passed which meant that Liversedge remained a township and the necessary works were started to provide water and to drain the whole town with main sewers and sewerage works.

The Drainage Works were formally opened by a Mr. Simon Kellett who was presented with a gold key in honour of the occasion!

Frank Peel has the last word as ever. He said that had the leading men of the Spen Valley been gifted with more foresight and had the wisdom to work together for a proper water supply and sewerage system instead of linking themselves to townships outside their limits, they would have saved a lot of arguments and unnecessary expense.

Urban District Councils Formed - 1884

Despite the obvious advantages of co-operation, the three towns remained fully independent and in 1884 they all three became Urban District Councils. They began providing other amenities.

By now the streets were lit by gas. Cleckheaton got its Public Baths. Heckmondwike was the first town in England to have Christmas Lights; the Illuminations in 1885! There was a growing pride in the towns.

Liversedge built its Town Hall at the top of Knowler Hill. Cleckheaton Council was also keen to build an impressive Town Hall and when Queen Victoria celebrated her Golden Jubilee in 1887, it gave them the reason for commemorating the event.

Cleckheaton Town Hall was ceremoniously opened in 1892 and became the centre-piece for the Spen Valley.

Better quality terraced houses were being built after 1890, such as the stylish stone- built houses on St Peg Lane.

Terrace Housing, Cleckheaton

Dealing With Disease

Even though there had been improvements made in Public Health, the living conditions of the vast majority were poor and infectious diseases spread quickly in areas of such dense population.

In 1854, the workhouse at Staincliffe opened. The district it covered was large; Batley, Morley, Dewsbury, Ossett, Mirfield, Thornhill, Soothill as well as Heckmondwike, Liversedge and Cleckheaton.

In 1884, four hospital wards were built within the workhouse and in 1894, an Infirmary was built with 200 beds.

Infirmaries were a new development. Until 1850, there were few around. Sick people from the Spen region would have to travel to Huddersfield or Leeds if they could afford the treatment.

After 1850, the need for hospitals became urgent with the spread of infectious diseases and problems from industrial accidents. Dewsbury, Batley and Mirfield all built small Voluntary Hospitals paid for by the community and by constant fundraising. Patients still had to pay for their treatment.

The hospital at Staincliffe however, was a Municipal Hospital, supported by public funds. It became the nucleus of Staincliffe General Hospital (now Dewsbury and District Hospital). The use of anaesthetics and better knowledge of basic surgical techniques meant that surgery could now be practised more safely in the new hospitals rather than before when surgery was performed by unqualified practitioners in patients' own homes.

Because infectious diseases were so deadly, patients with scarlet fever, diptheria, meningitis, smallpox, typhoid and dysentery were sometimes nursed in Isolation Hospitals which were made mandatory by Act of Parliament by the end of the century. The nearest for Spen folk was at North Bierley (on the site of the old manor house of the Richardson Family.)

As late as 1892 there were serious epidemics of smallpox and typhoid. It was in that year that the isolation hospital was built at North Bierley. A mortuary was added in 1898!

Life expectancy was still low and new cemeteries had to be provided; the first being in 1852 at Whitcliffe Road, Cleckheaton, covering 4 acres. In 1860 a cemetery was opened in Heckmondwike on a 6 acre site. In 1903 a cemetery at Liversedge was opened on a 12 acre site on Clough Lane along with a further site on Whitechapel Road, for Cleckheaton.

CHANGING TOWNSCAPES

CLECKHEATON

In the last quarter of the 19th Century, Northgate was transformed from the narrow dirty thoroughfare called Tofts Lane into a main street with new buildings and shops.

Two local architects were responsible for the fine Victorian buildings of the town; William Howorth and Reuben Castle.

The first building on Northgate from this era was Barclays Bank, built as the Lancashire and Yorkshire Bank in 1898 by William Henry Howorth.

Barclays Bank, Cleckheaton.

Reuben Castle built the Liberal Club, Churchill House also on Northgate. This was on the site of a Wesleyan Chapel which was too small for the growing congregation so had been re-built on Whitcliffe Road. (The cobbles and flagstones in front of Churchill House are all that remain of the chapel building). The Liberal Club included two billiard rooms, a news room and a large lecture and recreation room which could hold 200 people. Streets leading from the left of Northgate led to the Railway Station.

The three storey Cooperative Building graced Market Street where the open air market was held and nearby The George Inn remained the social centre of the town. The Public Baths on Tofts Street were very popular with showers and vapour baths in addition to the swimming baths.

The Town Hall, of course, was the most prestigious building in Cleckheaton. It had a large public hall for concerts and public meetings and plenty of office accommodation.

Town Hall, Cleckheaton

HECKMONDWIKE

Heckmondwike had new building work too. These included shops and banks.

Heckmondwike got its first charter for a Saturday market as early as 1810 and in 1880, a second charter allowed a market to be held on Tuesdays.

Heckmondwike now established its position as a market town and this encouraged even more commercial activity. And in the Market Place, an ornate drinking fountain was erected by public subscription to commemorate the marriage of the Prince and Princess of Wales, in 1863.

LIVERSEDGE AND GOMERSAL

The two oldest towns of the Spen Valley, Liversedge and Gomersal had, by the 19th Century, lost their dominance.

Both were dispersed settlements without an obvious nucleus. Both sat on high ridges which meant they had lost the benefits of water powered and steam powered mills which were built in the valley.

In fact, this statement appeared in Bradford Argus 1893, *'There is no such place as Liversedge.'*

Because whereas in earlier centuries, Liversedge was the most populous and important township, by the end of the 19th Century it had faded to comparative obscurity and it was difficult to see where its boundaries lay.

Millbridge was still the industrial heart of Liversedge and there was still a corn mill there, not the original medieval one, but one built in the late 18th Century.

But there was no village green or market street; only scattered centres like Littletown, Millbridge, Hightown, Roberttown and Norristhorpe.

There was a Town Hall but it didn't stand in the middle of a town!

Liversedge Town Hall

Gomersal too was without an obvious centre.

The township map of 1839 shows a cluster of shops at Hill Top on Oxford Road and at the junction with Knowles Lane but there were no obvious boundaries.

Interestingly, the Gomersal Tithe Map and Tithe Book of 1891 show the Masters, Fellows and Scholars of Trinity College Cambridge still owned the old glebe lands of Birstall.

So still a lot of historic baggage with the two oldest settlements.

THE NEW MARKET TOWNS

Cleckheaton and Heckmondwike, on the other hand, were down in the Spen Valley and attracted the mills and mill cottages.

They became the new market towns with all the shops and amenities needed by the growing population. They developed round a nucleus which made them well defined.

19th Century photographs of Cleckheaton and Heckmondwike show thriving towns bustling with people.

There were banks and building societies. The streets had been lit by gaslight since 1868 and were filled with horse drawn carts and people rushing to and from the railway stations.

They were full of shops like the Industrial Co-operative Societies. These were the largest shops of the day. They specialised in different commodities. There would be a Co-op. butchers, a haberdasherers, a grocers etc.

The Heckmondwike Co-op. was founded in the 1860's and opened a huge shop on the Green in 1871. There was a library and reading room and offices on the second floor. Gomersal had four Co-ops and Cleckheaton had several.

Cleckheaton had the massive frontage of Freeman Hardy and Willis' Shoe Emporium and the Lions Store started by John Wesley Hillard in 1885.

There were also lots of smaller specialist shops in both the towns and villages; cobblers, drapers, grocers, bakers and butchers.

In addition, there were lots of Corner Shops. These were the main shops for everyday shopping because people did not have the spare time to travel far because of their long hours of work.

They didn't have the money for transport and more importantly they needed to shop daily for food if they wanted their food fresh. These shops provided for all their needs.

So, one of the biggest developments in shopping habits was the growth of the corner shop which was literally at the corner of a row of terraced houses and therefore often outside the town centres.

It usually had two windows facing the two streets either side.

Corner shop, Cleckheaton

There were plenty of clubs; the Conservative and Liberal Clubs (no Labour Party yet), and Working Men's Clubs.

There were also plenty of pubs....

The Gray Ox Hartshead

The Rose & Crown, Westgate, Cleckheaton

Heckmondwike had The Duke William and The Woodman. Littletown had the Old Oak and The Swan. Gomersal had The White Horse and The Shoulder of Mutton. Little Gomersal had The Wheatsheaf and Spen had The Saw.

The Rising Sun and The Packhorse served the people of Scholes and The Black Bull was the heart of Millbridge. The Shears and The Cross Keys were two of the many inns along Halifax Road in Liversedge. The Star was the popular Roberttown pub and The Gray Ox, the social hub of Hartshead.

The Commercial was built in the 1830's in Cleckheaton and The George remained the centre of the town whilst one of the oldest inns was The Rose & Crown on Westgate.

LEISURE

Much of the leisure activity of the Spen Valley centred on the chapels and churches but there were plenty of clubs and pubs for those who neglected their vows of temperance! There were also seasonal events to look forward to like the annual fair.

Fairs

Heckmondwike Fair was held on the village green in the first weekend in May. There would be lots of sideshows and roundabouts, coconut shies and hoopla, brandy snap stalls and pie and pea stalls and lots of music and the dazzling lights from the steam engines. A photograph from 1889 shows a swing boat called the Swiss High Flyers and a Marionette show.

The Gomersal Fair was held in March and the Cleckheaton Fair in July on the Feast Ground (which was turned into a park in the following century).

The Hightown Rant was the highlight of the year for many Liversedge folk. This was a feast held in June in the field behind The Shears Inn.

Trips to the Seaside

Now that the railways provided cheap travel; many people went to Blackpool, Morecambe or Scarborough. Families booked a bedroom in advance and then took every item of food; meat, eggs, bacon, bread and butter, packed into a tin trunk and handed them over to their landlady when they arrived.

Children's Games

These were noted for being seasonal and costing hardly anything! At Easter, whips and tops, shuttlecocks and marbles appeared everywhere. Children drew circles with coloured chalk on the tops so that when they spun them on the pavement, they were a blur of colour. Skipping games and cricket became the craze in summer and on dark winter evenings, it was gas lamp swinging and hide and seek!

The Roberttown Races

One of the highlights of the year was the Roberttown Races. They actually started in the 1780's. By the early 19th Century they were well established and took place on Peep Green, then an open tract of common land.

This was an important village event for Roberttown and lasted three days in the middle of summer. The course stretched from the bottom of Low Common road by The Star Inn to The Grey Ox. On each side of the course were booths selling drinks among the crowds of spectators.

At Prospect House (on Prospect Lane), it's possible to see the railings on the roof where some people got a grandstand view as the horses galloped up from Low Common and on to The Grey Ox. At one point, the course crossed the old Leeds-Huddersfield road and one year a fatal accident occurred when horses were in collision with a fully loaded wagon. This ended the Roberttown Races but smaller local races were run for a few years and then the event gradually evolved into a country fair.

The Peep Green Fairs on the commons were very popular and only ended with the Enclosure Act of 1842 which privatised the land (following on from the Chartist meetings there).

In 1897, the inhabitants of the Spen Valley, like those throughout the land, celebrated Queen Victoria's Diamond Jubilee. A tower was built on Castle Hill and beacons were lit and there were many celebrations.

The century had seen massive changes in society and industry. But revolution had been avoided.

In 1900, one of our best known local historians, Frank Peel, died. His grave can be seen in Heckmondwike Cemetery. He had written about the changes caused by the Industrial Revolution so that his generation would remember what the Spen Valley used to be like. He would have been amazed by the speed of change in the century which followed.

Frank Peel's grave, Heckmondwike Cemetery

CHAPTER 12: THE 20th CENTURY

THE SPEN VALLEY IN THE TWO WORLD WARS

The impact of the two World Wars dominated the first half of the 20th Century.

The First World War was a war in which for the first time ordinary people from ordinary communities made up the armies of each of the nations at war.

Men who lived in the same street and who worked at the same factory and played in the same sports team, joined up together. They fought and too often died together.

Women were left to do the men's work at home and they too proved themselves in a war which was to involve the whole population, for the first time in history. They did the same again in the Second World War with the difference that many women were engaged in active service or working on the land as Land Girls.

Men and women shared the great and terrible communal experiences of war.

THE FIRST WORLD WAR 1914-1918

THE WESTERN FRONT

1914

From the start there was a swift and enthusiastic call to arms in the Spen Valley. Over a thousand men had enlisted by Christmas 1914.

There was a warm welcome for the Belgian refugees who escaped from their country when it was invaded by the Kaiser's army.

1915

Some of the first to go to the Front in 1915 were the Cleckheaton Territorials of the Duke of Wellington's 4th West Riding Regiment. (the regular army had been nearly eliminated by the fighting at the end of 1914). They were sent to France.

John Hirst, son of the owner of the Spenborough Guardian was a Private in the Regiment under the command of Captain Mowat from Kenmore, Cleckheaton.

They were given a great send off from Doncaster station in April 1915. Among them was the priest of St Saviour's Church in Heckmondwike.

Other local men joined battalions which served in different areas of the war.

Corporal Haldenby of Clare Street, Cleckheaton, won the DSM in April 1915 at the Battle of Hill 60 in Belgium. Battalion Sergeant Major Chadwick, an old boy of Moorbottom National School fought at Gallipoli in Turkey.

The carnage on the Western Front continued throughout 1915 and the introduction of poisonous gas and flame throwers into the arsenal of new weaponry added to the terrors of fighting in the trenches.

John Hirst wrote graphic accounts of the horrors he saw for his father's newspaper. These, together with letters sent from the Front, provided Andrew Bannister with some remarkable background material for his book, 'One Valley's War.'

War weariness had set in by the second Christmas. But the following year saw the introduction, for the first time, of conscription.

This was now a necessity due to the heavy casualties.

221

1916

The First Fourth was in the thick of the fighting at the Battle of the Somme from July to November 1916.

Long lists of casualties filled the columns of the local newspapers. The Battalion was now fighting with the Bradford Pals and the Leeds Pals.

The worst day for casualties was the 3rd of September which, by bitter irony, was a local holiday back home. They were involved in an attack on a stretch of land between the French villages of Gommecourt and Thiepval.

1917

This year saw more slaughter at the Battle of Passchendale in Belgium when the British advanced seven miles in four months losing a quarter of a million men. The survivors of that ordeal were back in the Spring of 1918 at the Third Battle of Ypres.

And the carnage went on.

THE WAR AT SEA

The Spen Valley was well represented in the War at Sea and some local men took part in the major sea battle at Jutland in 1916 when several lost their lives, among them Arthur Worthington of Wyke, Thomas Blakely (who was only sixteen years old) and Clifford Hirst, both from Heckmondwike and Henry Collett of Gomersal.

German submarines caused havoc to merchant ships and naval ships alike and in 1915 were responsible for the sinking of a passenger ship, the Lusitania when over a thousand people died. One of the lucky ones to survive was Olive North of Cambridge Street, Heckmondwike who actually went down with the ship but managed to grasp hold of a lifeboat that had been capsized!

INDUSTRY

The war brought about a great upheaval in society, particularly for women. At first it was considered inappropriate for married women to go out to work and leave their children. Unmarried women were already working in the factories or in domestic service. But as more and more men left for the Front, women were needed to fill their jobs and particularly in the munitions factories.

Industry flourished in the Spen Valley during the war and products made locally played an important part in the war effort; army uniforms, barbed wire, lyddite, motor cycles, gas for smoke screens, among others.

Only the coal mining industry suffered because many miners saw the army and the navy as a way of escaping from their dangerous jobs! The miners who did stay, fought hard for better wages and working conditions. In 1916 those at White Lee Colliery actually went on strike. Later that year strikes were made illegal for the duration of the war.

It was left to the Trades Unions in the Spen Valley to make sure that workers were rewarded for their extra efforts. There was a widespread feeling that the employers were gaining much more from the full order books than their workforces.

Munitions work was often very dangerous and two particularly horrific accidents occurred; one in December 1914 when ten men were killed in an explosion in the pitric acid works at White Lee and one in August 1916, when forty people were killed in an explosion which devastated the munitions works at Low Moor.

CHANGES IN SOCIETY

Women as well as men worked in dangerous conditions. Their contribution to the war effort led to a changing perception of their roles in society.

In 1903, the Suffragette Movement was founded and their members, trying to get the vote for women, were becoming increasingly desperate in their actions. They were even suspected of planting a bomb at the Dewsbury and Heckmondwike water board reservoir at Dunford Bridge in 1914.

Such action was not likely to get them the vote, but the war changed all that and women were seen in a new light. In 1919, the vote was given to women over the age of thirty and in 1928, to all women over the age of twenty-one.

When the First World War finally ended in 1918, the rejoicing in the Spen Valley was tinged with great sorrow. Most families had lost loved ones.

The First Fourth returned from France in June 1919. Lieutenant-Colonel Mowat, (one of the few original members to return) and his men were given an official welcome home. The servicemen marched behind the First Fourth band through Cleckheaton. The town was filled with people and the streets were decorated with bunting.

A large sign simply said; *'Spenborough Thanks You All.'*

CHANGES IN POLITICS BETWEEN THE WARS

The 20th Century saw the emergence of the Socialist or Labour Party and the decline of the Liberal Party. Until this time, the two main Parties were the Conservatives and the Liberals. The Spen Valley had a tradition of voting for the Liberals. The new Labour Party was given a boost in 1911 when MPs were given a salary for the first time, thus allowing working men to be elected.

This meant that in 1918 when the war ended and a General Election could be held, a Labour candidate was put forward for the first time in the Spen Valley. This was Tom Myers (whose name graces the local Labour Party Offices in Cleckheaton).

His rival, Sir Thomas Whitaker, the well respected Liberal incumbent, tried to convince voters that Myers had not been supportive enough of the war effort. But despite these slurs and the fact that Whitaker was a well known figure, Myers got plenty of votes from the working classes (which now included a large number of women.) Tom Myers used the argument that only working class MPs could understand the problems of the electorate. He was only narrowly defeated.

The following year a bye-election was called following the death of Sir Thomas Whitaker. This time there were three candidates: Sir John Simon, the Liberal candidate, who used 104 cars (cars!) to get people to the polling stations; Lt. Colonel Bryan Charles Fairfax, the Coalition candidate, who used 54 cars for that purpose and Tom Myers who used 7. The result of the election announced in January 1920 was that the Spen Valley had got its first Labour MP!

The First World War had changed the outlook and aspirations of people living in the Spen Valley as it did throughout the country.

THE SECOND WORLD WAR 1939-1945

Twenty one years later another world war broke out.

This was different from the first because of the threat of bombing from the air. During the First World War, there was no real danger from the German Zeppelins' bombing the towns of the Spen Valley as they could only fly as far as the coastline.

A year before war broke out, the Spenborough Guardian ran an article explaining that, *'ARP work in the Spen Valley is proceeding smoothly. Warning sirens were successfully tested on Wednesday. Trenches will accommodate nearly 4,000 residents in Spenborough and about 1,000 in Heckmondwike.'* It mentioned that, *'There is an anti-aircraft observation post in Heckmondwike.'* and that, *'During the week, the distribution of gas masks has been carried out.'*

That was September 30th 1938. Once war was declared on Sunday 3rd September 1939, life changed. For the first time in history, civilians were under attack from enemy bombing. The war had come to the people at home. They were part of the war, the Home Front. Their priorities were to stay alive and to meet the demands of war. They were also under far more Government control than ever before.

THE HOME FRONT

Now there had to be measures put into place to counter-attack the war from the air.

Total black out was one of these measures. Every night Air Raid Wardens ensured that not one chink of light escaped from windows and doors. Offenders were taken to court and fined. There were no street lights. Lamp posts and kerb edges were painted with white paint.

When air raids did occur, everyone had to dash to an air raid shelter as soon as the air raid sirens sounded. One woman from Cleckheaton explained how you had to have your clothes piled up ready before you went to bed in case you had to run to the shelter and how for years afterwards she couldn't break this habit.

Luckily there was no serious bombing in the area but as this was the main route to Bradford, Leeds, Manchester and Liverpool, there were plenty of bombers droning in the skies overhead, particularly between the summers of 1940 and 1941 when the major cities were bombed.

Incendiary bombs were a serious hazard and after 1941 all workers had to take part in fire watching at public buildings and industrial buildings. Also in 1941, five hundred women and children were evacuated to the Spen Valley from cities which were experiencing large scale bombing.

They were billeted mainly with working class families because as a WVS officer said, *'People in big houses don't want their serenity disturbed!'*

CIVIL DEFENCE

Each neighbourhood in the Spen Valley had its own network of Civil Defence personnel. There was the fire service, rescue, ambulance, ARP, and WVS. They went on duty every night after their day jobs. There were many local men who worked long hours in reserved occupations who went on patrol in the Home Guard or as Special Constables.

MUNITIONS WORK

The Government organised the country as one big work force. People were ordered to work in a specific place of work and this could be anywhere in the British Isles.

Some men were exempted from conscription if they were involved in war work and women were forced into this work particularly after 1941 when increased industrial production was urgently needed. In the Spen Valley this involved the manufacture of, among other things, uniforms and blankets and components for tanks and aircraft and radios. Textiles, engineering and chemical factories all concentrated their production on war supplies. The Government provided nursery schools for the children of mothers doing war work.

THE ROLE OF WOMEN

As in the First World War, women filled the places of men in the mills, doing work which had previously been considered men's work. And now for the first time, women who did not have families were conscripted, like the men, into the Armed Forces.

They were given the option of the Women's Auxilliary Services, (ATS-army, WAAF-airforce, or WRNS-navy), Civil Defence or the Women's Land Army.

Many local women had to live away from home. Some women took on jobs which must have seemed impossible in the days before the war,

For example, Nellie Jackson of Littletown became Spen's first signalwoman when she changed jobs from a goods porter on the railways to take over the signal box at Liversedge Spen Station.

The whole population was organised for the war effort and class divisions were broken down as everyone worked together for the common good.

RATIONING

Rationing had to be introduced, as in the previous war, so that everyone had an equal share of food. This time it was from the start of the war. People were encouraged to be self sufficient and grow some of their own food in allotments.

The Spenborough Dig for Victory Campaign, organised by the Allotments Committee, rented allotments out and organised lectures, such as one held at Gomersal Public Hall on the subject of, *'The uses of various manures and how they should be applied.'*

Gardens were dug up too so that food could be grown to supplement the meagre food rations. The only thing not rationed was bread but the National Loaf was made with lots of salt to help preserve it and so it was not popular. In fact it was often referred to as, *'Hitler's secret weapon.'*

The Ministry of Food organised food demonstrations such as the one at Cleckheaton Town Hall entitled, *'New ways of cooking vegetables.'*

Most local people welcomed rationing because everyone got the same and they did get a balanced diet. There was a good spirit of sharing and swapping of coupons. Even so, there were an awful lot of advertisements for indigestion tablets in local newspapers!

If certain items of food were not available, it was no use grumbling. In December 1943, the Spenborough Guardian stated that there were only enough turkeys for, *'one in ten families.'*

MAKE DO AND MEND

Make Do And Mend became another strategy of the war effort. The few goods in the shops were drab and utilitarian and there were no non-essential products like toys. Fathers had to make wooden toys for their children and the children themselves had to be far more creative with their play.

Of more importance was the need to clothe your family. From 1941, clothes were rationed so make do and mend classes were held at local schools.

One woman from Hightown remembers always patching and mending clothes. Then her husband changed jobs and got a bit more more money so she treated herself to some basic underwear which had become something of a luxury! Many local people hadn't enough money to actually use their food or clothing coupons.

Dance halls and cinemas were the popular places to escape from the war and the community spirit in the valley was very strong. This was the first time that war had been brought home to the civilian populations.

Everyone was involved. But this meant that people talked to each other and helped each other. They were all in it together.

LOCAL PEOPLE

Local people contributed to the Spenborough Forget Me Not Fund and they donated £5,000 for a Spitfire aeroplane.

The fund had been started in 1915 during the 1st World War by Alfred Hirst, a former Scout Master of the Moorbottom troop. This involved sending Christmas cards and gifts and regular parcels to the armed forces. This was re-established in October 1939 and throughout the war all kinds of activities were organised to raise funds (and of course it still exists).

Some families endured six years of unimaginable worry and stress.

Local newspapers mention Mr. and Mrs. Walker of Oxford Road Gomersal who had four sons serving in the armed forces in 1941. Mr. and Mrs. Bridges of Strawberry Bank, Liversedge, had six of their seven sons serving in 1942 and Mr. and Mrs. Biddle of Millbridge had three sons and a daughter serving abroad in the same year.

There are very few accounts of wartime activities in the newspapers because of the need for censorship but in May 1940 there is an account of two men from Cleckheaton, Flt Lt. Albert Kaye and Gunner Herbert Simper who wrote about their harrowing escape from the Norwegian fiords.

And home on leave in 1940 , after experiencing a German bombing raid at sea was Arthur Yeadon, a twenty-eight year old wireless operator of Park Street Gomersal who told of his ordeal as his tanker was, *'Almost dashed to bits.'*

In 1941 seven local sailors were serving on the battleships Repulse and the Prince of Wales when their ships were sunk by the Japanese off the coast of Malaya.

Gunner Jack Anall of Union Road, Liversedge, took part in the D-Day landings and brought himself and his crew members, including his mortally wounded tank commander, to safety. Afterwards he said, *'What I did was nothing.'*

Every week the Spenborough Guardian printed its Roll of Honour. This included not only the dead, but those reported missing and those who were Prisoners of War, as well as those who had received a medal for bravery.

One of the first to be mentioned was Tom Hoggard of Hunsworth who received the DFM whilst serving as a wireless operator. He was promoted from Corporal to Sergeant as a result.

In July 1940, a twenty three year old Scholes man, Sapper James Barber of the Royal Engineers was recorded missing. The report added that his father lost his life in the last war.

Ronald Smith of Cleckheaton was wounded while serving on one of the British ships engaged in the sinking of the German battleship the Bismarck and he was mentioned as being in a military hospital in (occupied) Northern France. Gunner Jim Helliwell from Scholes sent a photo of himself with other POWs in Germany and said he was putting his knowledge of German to good use by acting as an interpreter. The Roll of Honour grew longer and longer as the war progressed. Many made the ultimate sacrifice.

Cleckheaton War Memorial (Re-dedication Ceremony)

The war had been life changing for everyone, both at home and abroad, and long after the victory celebrations had been held in the Spen Valley, a lot of adjustments had to be made from such a long period of hardship.

THE FIVE GIANTS

Following the war, the Spen Valley returned a Labour candidate for the first time in a General Election. And with a majority of 6,077!

The feeling here as in many parts of the country was that the Labour Party was the Party which would help the working classes.

Just as the Liberal Government had promised a Land Fit For Heroes in 1918, so the new Labour Government, elected in 1945, promised to provide a better and fairer Britain.

It was about to slay the Five Giants of: Want, Disease, Squalor, Idleness and Ignorance.

These promises were carried out in the years after the war. The National Insurance Act dealt with want, the National Health Act with disease, the building of council houses with squalor, the creation of jobs with idleness and the 1944 Education Act with ignorance.

Here in the Spen Valley we were to see the benefits of all five 'slayings.' The Government was building on all that had been learnt during the war and using it to build a Welfare State.

Reforms on such a scale had been impossible following the First World War because of the world wide recession in the 1930's.

But now, socialist ideas were able to develop and grow, creating a much fairer society.

CHAPTER 13: LOCAL GOVERNMENT IN THE 20th CENTURY AND BEYOND

PUBLIC HEALTH AND EDUCATION

The two World Wars had an enormous impact on the way in which central government developed. We can now look back and see how local government developed in the Spen Valley throughout the 20th Century.

During the previous century, the Local Boards had been the predecessors of the Urban District Councils, which were set up in 1884, and despite the obvious benefits of a unified council, the different parts of the Spen Valley remained stubbornly separate.

At the start of the 20th Century, efforts were made to improve the centres of each township. In 1902, Public Baths were opened as well as a Fire Station in Heckmondwike. In 1904, Heckmondwike residents paid for a clock to be added to the beautiful drinking fountain in the Market Place.

A Public Library was built in 1907, the site being given to the town by Sir Thomas Firth. And the village green was transformed into a little park in 1912 to commemorate the Coronation of King George V.

Before this time, Green Park had been part of the original green which had stretched from Oldfield Lane to the Flush.

It was the Heckmondwike District Co-operative Society which decided to create the park not only to celebrate the coronation but to beautify the town at the same time. The Co-op gave £150 towards the new park and the rest of the money was raised by public subscription.

Cleckheaton also continued to make changes. The Town Hall became the centerpiece for the Spen Valley and many organizations used it.

In 1908, Emily Pankhurst and other Suffragettes visited and gave speeches here about their struggle to achieve Votes for Women.

The feast ground in Cleckheaton was transformed into the Edward VII Memorial Park in 1912. It was laid out with flower beds and surrounded by railings. The main feature was a bandstand where brass bands regularly played. That is until 1922 when it was replaced by the War Memorial which was dedicated by Lieutenant Colonel Mowat. This memorial remembered the names of the 470 men from the Spen Valley who had died in the First World War.

After the Second World War, a further 218 names were added and on June 27th 2009, the memorial was re-dedicated by Colonel Mowat's grandson; Major General Jonathan Shaw, son of Lord and Lady Shaw of Duxbury Hall, Roberttown. Seven more names were added to the War Memorial. These were the men who had died in wars following the Second World War. The Mowat Family was also responsible for Cleckheaton Library opened in 1930 in Whitcliffe Road, Cleckheaton.

Memorial Park, Cleckheaton

THE SPEN URBAN DISTRICT: SPENBOROUGH

In 1915, the inevitable happened and the three councils of Liversedge, Cleckheaton and Gomersal (not Heckmondwike) united and became the Spen Urban District or Spenborough.

By 1937, the Urban Districts of Birkenshaw, Hunsworth and Hartshead had been added. Heckmondwike still retained its independence.

In 1955, the Spen Urban District Council gained Borough status which meant it now had a Mayor.

Then in 1974, everything changed again.

KIRKLEES METROPOLITAN COUNCIL AND NORTH KIRKLEES

Kirklees Metropolitan Council was formed under local government re-organisation.

All the Urban Districts were to be run from Huddersfield. Forty councilors would represent the Spen region and twelve would represent, Heckmondwike, which finally lost its independent status. The Spen Valley was now part of North Kirklees.

The consequences were far reaching.

A great deal of civic pride disappeared and some felt that it became more difficult to keep in touch with councillors and that the personal touch had been lost.

It was certainly no longer local government as people had known it.

Local Government is responsible for many aspects of life but two are crucial; Public Health and Education. We can see the developments of each of these as the century progressed.

PUBLIC HEALTH

The effects of the Industrial Revolution in terms of poor housing and widespread disease did not improve very much. The services of rat catchers like Thomas Cassidy of Heckmondwike were still in demand!

The Advertiser and Times announced action taken by the Spenborough Urban District Council against an epidemic of smallpox as late as November 1928.

The economic depression of the 1920's and 1930's did not help the situation and whilst some people became very wealthy because of the growth of new industries, the vast majority earned barely enough to live on.

HOUSING

Living conditions remained poor for most people. Homes were rented and were still overcrowded, with outside toilets and no electricity.

Many houses only consisted of two rooms. The living room downstairs led directly on to the street and had a sink in the corner, and a fireplace. Upstairs was the one square bedroom. And this was the space in which a large family was brought up.

CHANGES FOLLOWING THE FIRST WORLD WAR

The drive for change was led by the trade unions, by town councils and occasionally by far sighted individuals, the entrepreneurs who involved themselves, as ever, in problems concerning the community.

One example of these was Sir Algernon Firth, the owner of Flush Mill in Heckmondwike. He was already involved in a pioneering model housing scheme for his workers in the United States where he had built a mill.

He called this village (near New York), Firthcliffe, and he had similar ideas for Heckmondwike.

He laid his plans before Heckmondwike Urban District Council in August 1918. He wanted well built houses so that the days of cramped and insanitary homes would be over.

Many people in fact now recognised the effects of poor housing on health. Too many soldiers had been rejected by the medical boards in 1914 as being unfit to serve their country.

In 1918, there was a feeling that the soldiers who did return from the Great War, should return to a land fit for heroes.

Sir Algernon Firth argued for more planning so that people did not live in the valley in close proximity to the mills, but on the hillsides. He urged the local authorities in the Spen Valley to set to work to make this not only an ideal district for the manufacturing industries but also for the workers who lived there!

The idea of local authority housing was a new one but Spenborough Urban District Council and Heckmondwike Council realised that it was their duty to provide the urgently needed housing. This was very much overdue.

In 1919, a labour councilor, (soon to be MP) Tom Myers, found that the Spen Valley was one of the worst in Yorkshire for housing standards. There were far too many houses with fewer than three rooms in which to bring up a large family.

When Spenborough and Heckmondwike Councils started providing Corporation Houses in the 1920's, facilities were much improved. Examples of these are the Firthcliffe Estate in Liversedge built between 1923 and 1924 on land donated by Sir Algernon Firth, and the Shirley Estate in Gomersal for many of Burnleys' workforce. By the 1940's most homes had electricity. This was a start.

Firthcliffe Estate, Littletown, Liversedge

CHANGES AFTER THE SECOND WORLD WAR

It was only after the Second World War, however that things really began to improve.

This time reform was carried out by the Labour Party; the Party which had taken over from the Liberals as the Party trying to improve life for the working classes. The Labour Government which came into office in 1945, put into place a Welfare State and a major programme of slum clearance and house -building. This was the Giant Squalor which it was committed to slaying!

The erection of back-to-back houses had been made illegal in 1909 because it was finally realised that such housing caused too much congestion and too many health problems.

But there were still many areas filled with this type of housing. Slum clearance was now a top priority for local government.

Followed by the building of new houses.

In 1945, Spen's biggest housing development began. The Windy Bank Estate was to have 554 houses, shops and a community centre.

Interestingly, it was a gang of thirty German prisoners of war who were brought in to dig out the site and build the eighteen roads which made up the estate. At least one of these POWs stayed on after the war.

One lady remembers going to get milk from a farm near the estate and being served by a German who had married the farmer's daughter.

Windy Bank Estate, Hightown

By 1959, nearly 1,000 houses had been demolished and 893 council houses and 468 private houses had been built.

Other changes were equally dramatic.

In the 1960's, the village of Littletown disappeared as a dual carriageway swept across the heart of the village with its village green and little shops. A once thriving community had gone.

Also in the 1960's, the massive Central Chapel in Cleckheaton was demolished and a Post Office built on the site.

Other new buildings included children's nurseries, health centres and old people's homes.

More housing estates followed, some on the sites of former mills and millowners' homes such as the Bridon Estate, where Pyenot Hall once stood with its stone lion which perched on an archway to the Hall.

'Yon Lion' has been given a new home on the estate thanks to the Spen Valley Civic Society.

A nice link with the old and the new.

In 2010 a £15 million scheme by Yorkshire Water was completed. This involved laying an 8 mile sewer pipe between Heckmondwike and the Water Treatment Works at Mitchell Laithes.

This was part of a wider £90 million investment by the company to improve the quality of the water in the rivers Spen and Calder to a standard not seen since before the industrial revolution.

Frank Peel would no doubt have approved!

THE NATIONAL HEALTH SERVICE

Perhaps the biggest landmark of the 20th Century was the 1946 National Health Act setting up the National Health Service. This set out the blueprint for regional Hospital Boards to plan and manage hospitals. It also set up Executive Councils to administer medical, dental, pharmaceutical and optical services.

There were also to be County Borough Councils to provide community health services. And at first it was all to be free! People rushed to get spectacles and sets of false teeth and all their ailments sorted out and the doctors were rushed off their feet!

Staincliffe hospital was now transferred to the NHS. New buildings were added in the 1960's and in the 1980's the old workhouse building was finally demolished and its site was used to build the Priestley Mental Health Unit.

Health care has come a long way and hospitals like Staincliffe, (Dewsbury and District Hospital) which now serves the whole region, have highly technical procedures which diagnose and treat diseases which in previous centuries had not even been recognised.

There are community services supported by GP's and Primary Health Care centre teams looking after us all. People are living longer and healthier lives.

And one Liversedge man, Robert Corry, played a significant role in this progress. He made the titanium frame of the valve, first used in heart surgery here and abroad.

There are still problems despite all the money spent on health services but the priority health issues are now obesity and high rates of heart disease, high blood pressure and lung cancer. These are very different problems from those of the past.

EDUCATION

One thing the Second World War did was to highlight the unfairness of the educational system. For most children a secondary education was not possible. They went to school from the ages of five to fourteen and had no specialist subject knowledge.

THE 1944 EDUCATION ACT

In 1944, before the war was over, a new system was designed so that all children would be given a Secondary Education after the age of eleven in one of three types of school; Grammar, Technical and Secondary Modern.

The first would cater for academic pupils, the second for those wishing to learn science and engineering and a trade and the third for those who wished to do manual work. Provision was made to move between the three but in order to get into the Grammar School, pupils must pass the 11+ Examination.

The school leaving age was raised to fifteen although for Grammar Schools it was sixteen and more often eighteen. This all required the building of more and more schools.

In the 1950's and 1960's there were new schools built in the Spen Valley, as well as all the housing. There were already two Grammar Schools, at Whitcliffe Mount and Heckmondwike Grammar School.

In 1957, a County Secondary School was opened at Roberttown to take pupils from Liversedge and Heckmondwike.

In 1960 another County Secondary School was opened in Birkenshaw serving Gomersal, East Bierley, Hunsworth and Birkenshaw.

There was already a Secondary School on South Parade in Cleckheaton. So five schools now catered for pupils over the age of eleven.

The Elementary Schools (The old Board Schools) were replaced by Infants and Junior Schools.

The first post-war school built in the Spen Valley was the Spenborough Gryllis Junior School on the Windy Bank Estate. The second, Royds Infants School Heckmondwike, was built in the same year, 1954. In the following year a new Infants School was built in Birkenshaw.

1974 THE COMPREHENSIVE SYSTEM

Then in 1974, the Comprehensive System of education was introduced and Cleckheaton adopted the Whitcliffe Mount Pyramid model.

This involved a three tier system whereby First Schools took children from 5 to 9 years and Middle Schools catered for the 9 to 13 year olds. Whitcliffe Mount lost its Grammar School status and became the Secondary School for the area.

This led to more school building.

The three tier system began showing its weaknesses at the start of the 21st Century and a move back to the two tier system was proving to be the preferred choice bringing it in line with most of the country.

This was to lead to heated debates when the separate communities strove to keep their schools until all was sorted out by 2012.

Liversedge and Heckmondwike adopted the two tier system from the start. This meant that there were infant and junior schools for children from 5 to 11 and after the age of eleven, children were educated at the secondary schools at Roberttown and Heckmondwike. These two schools merged in 1993 to become the Spen Valley Sports College in Roberttown.

Heckmondwike Grammar School remains a selective school serving the whole valley.

PLANNING FOR THE FUTURE

Local Government is now responsible for many other things besides health and education issues.

It has to address the new challenges which have arisen such as helping businesses and providing information and training for the unemployed due to globalisation in trade and commerce. It has to encourage people to use carbon cutting schemes because of climate change. This also involves reducing the need to travel by private car. It has to deal with the threat of flooding, and provide local flood defences.

It continues to regenerate our historic mill towns and villages.

In Heckmondwike, for example, improvements have been made to the Market Place and the street layout. The shops have smart new signages and canopies. A new bandstand graces the park, with a crown of lights in memory of the Christmas illuminations! This is happening all over the area and makes for a far more attractive environment for people to live in.

And what about Liversedge the oldest settlement?

It has become difficult to see where the boundaries now lie. The focal points of the Spen Valley are Heckmondwike and Cleckheaton. They are the centres for shops and financial services, health, leisure and entertainment. Only Roberttown remains as a village from the old Liversedge.

In an effort to redress this, the Spen Valley Civic Society has created a little park to celebrate the history of Liversedge as well as commemorating the activities of the Luddites two hundred years ago.

This is at the top of Knowler Hill, very near to the original centre of Liversedge as well as being close to the Hustings Knoll where the history of Liversedge began.

So now Liversedge has got its centre back, complete with an information board ensuring everyone knows they are in the town of Liversedge!

The demands of local government today are challenging.

There is the constant need for careful planning on issues of housing, health, employment, public transport, and education. Many of the requirements which have to be met come from central government and have to be squared with local feelings.

For example the need to plan for affordable housing, open spaces, sport and recreation as well as industrial development. This has to be done so that we protect the Green Belt as well as the integrity of existing villages.

Planning for housing and industrial building is important if we want to avoid the uncontrolled development of the past.

Local government officers claim to ensure that, *'Our towns and villages remain pleasant places to live for generations to come.'* (Local Development Planning for Jobs and Homes 2010)

This involves one of the biggest challenges; dealing with the blight caused by derelict areas which once formed the industrial backbone of the Spen Valley. It is hoped that whatever plans are made, they will always be underpinned by the principle of protecting those areas and buildings of historical importance which explain so much of the Spen Valley's rich history.

The identity of villages like Roberttown, Hartshead and Gomersal should always be safeguarded.

The landscape between the Three Nuns and the former Roe Head School, now Hollybank School, for example has the footprints of history from the 12th Century onwards and should be kept for future generations to enjoy.

CHAPTER 14: LIVING IN THE SPEN VALLEY IN THE 20th CENTURY AND BEYOND

The 20th Century was a century of rapid change.

Two world wars speeded up the momentum of change. We have looked at the ways in which central and local government extended their work and made long lasting changes in public health, housing and education. But equally, in no other century have there been such rapid changes in work and leisure.

We finish our story of the people of the Spen Valley by seeing how they lived through all these changes.

CHANGES IN LEISURE ACTIVITIES

The Cinema

The cinema became very popular at the start of the 20th Century and every town had one or two cinemas.

Heckmondwike's cinemas date from 1911 when the Palace Cinema was built on High Street and the Pavilion Cinema, in 1914, in Croft Street.

Cleckheaton's Picture Palace was opened in 1911 by local entrepreneur Walter Goodall and the Savoy Cinema next door, opened in 1923 was also part of his empire.

This seated 1,200 people. There were three shows on Saturdays including a matinee which was much loved by local children. People went to the cinema once or twice a week and some boasted an organ and for a time, an orchestra!

Cinemas became less popular with the advent of television and all the local ones closed in the 1960's.

But the site of the Savoy Cinema has been turned into a green oasis in the middle of Cleckheaton with a series of film posters, based on local historical events and painted by local artists, decorating the adjacent wall.

One of these advertises, *'SHIRLEY: A RED HOUSE MELODRAMA,'* a Taylor/ Briarmains Production

Another advertises: *'ATTACK ON RAWFOLDS MILL,'* starring George Mellor, John Booth, Samuel Hartley and William Cartwright: A Savoy Picture

This little park was planned by the Spen Valley Civic Society not only as an attractive amenity for the town but as a visual reminder of the cinema and of the history of Spen Valley.

At the corner of the park stands a cornerstone memorial to the local cinema with a plaque proclaiming, *'The Savoy Cinema stood here 1923– 1960. All that remains is this stone from the corner of Albion Street.'*

Cinema Memorial, Cleckheaton

Dancing

Before the Second World War, there was still very little free time for leisure. Hours were long and until 1937 there were no paid holidays. People made their own entertainment and socialising was still mainly done in the church and chapel functions.

One of the favourite social activities was dancing. Dance schools became popular, like the Stevenson Dance Academy on Moor Lane Gomersal, opened in 1910 by Tom and Emily Stevenson in the former silk mill, built and owned by the Porritt Family in 1825.

It was nicknamed Stivvy's and the old mill was transformed.

The ground floor housed the cloakroom, then steep stone steps led to the refreshment area (tea and coffee and biscuits included in the price of three pence). Another flight of steps led to the ballroom which had space for 300 dancers and was the height of luxury with a Canadian maple floor, comfy seats (bought from a closed-down Birstall cinema), wall mirrors and floodlighting.

It was very easy to get to Stivvy's as the tram between Bradford and Dewsbury stopped there and the Gomersal railway station was just across Moor Lane. It became a highly popular venue. In the 1920's there was a craze for marathon dancing. Couples danced for as long as possible and the winning pair was the last ones standing.

Thomas Harland and his partner Ethel Calvert took to the floor at 8 o'clock one evening and carried on dancing without a break for twelve hours and only stopped because the band ran out of accompanying musicians!

The 1950's saw the era of the Teddy Boys and the rock and roll craze continued well into the 1960's. Ballroom dancing was taught right from the start first by Tom and Emily Stevenson and after the 1940's by their daughter Dorothy, up to 1979.

The old silk mill has now been restored and a Dance School is once again using that magical space on the top floor. The lower floors are equally magical being stuffed full of beautiful antiques!

When you visit the upper floor in this little mill, you can still sense the feeling expressed by a local man born in 1922, *'Fantastic. You were in another world. Because you didn't venture much out of Gomersal. The only time you saw anything like that were in t'films. You saw the Waldorf Hotel and Paris and all those low cut frocks. And to go to Stivvy's and to have a live band and mirrors on't wall, you could see yourself dancing, how good you looked. Fantastic.'*

The Spen Valley remains a centre for dance schools, some of which have produced talented young people who have gone on to appear in musicals in different parts of the country.

Excursions to the Seaside

There were also excursions to the seaside. The mills closed down in Spen Week and most people went on special excursion trains to Blackpool. They would probably know everyone else on holiday there! Coach trips were now also very popular and coaches often picked up their passengers at the factory gates, the pub or sunday school to take them on holiday to the coast.

The Heckmondwike Illuminations

One event, held on Heckmondwike Green, drew crowds of people from miles around. This was the famous Heckmondwike Illuminations.

These became a major attraction from the 1930's when over twenty spectacular set pieces turned Heckmondwike into a magical fairy land! Special trains were laid on from all over West Yorkshire. They were possibly the very first Christmas illuminations and were the inspiration for the famous Blackpool Illuminations.

The second World War put a temporary stop to them but as soon as the wartime blackout ended, the lights went on, a welcome sight during the austerity years that followed the war.

The sets were based on nursery rhymes and pantomime characters and were a huge source of entertainment for all the family but for children they were the highlight of Christmas.

They watched with fascination as Cinderella waved at the crowds and the wheels of her golden coach turned round and round. A sea lion balanced a ball on its nose; and an elephant raised its illuminated trunk to the sky; a peacock's shimmering tail fanned outwards and two boxing cats danced on their hind legs. I remember it well!

There is now a Crown of Lights in the park to commemorate this wonderful event.

Cleckheaton Folk Festival

This started as a small affair in 1987 and it has grown to a large three day event at the beginning of July, attracting people from all over the world.

There are lots of folk singers and musicians but also workshops and fringe events, dance, street entertainment and a craft fair. The evening entertainment is based in the Town Hall but this spills over into the local pubs.

CHANGES IN TRANSPORT

Trams

The first serious rivals to the railways were the Trams. The tramcar depot was at Frost Hill, Liversedge and the Yorkshire Woollen District Electric Tramways Ltd started operating in 1905.

One of the comments displayed at the exhibition at the Red House Museum, shows how popular trams were, *'It used to cost a penny from Gomersal to Heckmondwike on't tram and a penny back, and it were worth every penny to come round t'swan corner sat upstairs ont back of a tram. It were real.'*

Trams had slatted wooden seats and there was a hand bell near the driver. At first the upper deck was open-topped. By the time of their demise, there were 82 trams, with regular services between the towns and villages.

Motor Buses and New Roads.

Trams were succeeded by the motor bus. The Daimler 16-seater arrived on the scene about 1912. J. Ramsden, a wheelwright from Millbridge began making 18-seater motor buses in 1924. Buses at first were operated by private family businesses but eventually the Yorkshire Heavy Woollen District Bus Company was established. The narrow roads with their cobbled surfaces were improved. New roads were built like Hightown Road in 1922. And old roads were widened where possible and tarmacadamed.

But maps of the time still show the main roads as narrow, insignificant thoroughfares and you need to peer very closely to identify them. The railways, on the other hand cut huge swathes across the maps and the map of the Spen Valley is covered with wide sweeping railway lines, railway stations and goods yards.

The End of Local Railway Lines

The railways were still very busy in the first half of the century. Local trains stopped at Heckmondwike, Cleckheaton, Liversedge and Gomersal. The Newcastle to Liverpool trains used to rattle through Gomersal station at 80 mph and passengers waiting on the platform for local trains had to stand well back!

This all ended with the Beeching Cuts of the 1960's. George Anderton's railway was one of the lines cut. The stations were dismantled and Cleckheaton viaduct fell into disuse.

Maps after the 1970's see a complete reversal.

The M62 Motorway and the M606 replace the dominance that the railways once had. The major roads are quite clearly the busy arteries of transport. The M62 was built in 1972 and passes through Spenborough. Motorways have a dramatic effect on the landscape.

Other road improvements have also had their consequences, for example in 1970, the dual carriageway linking Cleckheaton and Liversedge opened. This widened the existing road at the expense of the village of Littletown.

The former railway tracks have to be searched for now on local maps because they are now shown as the Greenway for walkers and cyclists to use at a more leisurely pace.

CHANGES IN RELIGION

Church and Chapel

As England became more and more of a secular country, the Spen Valley followed the trend. There was a gradual decline in church and chapel going, particularly from the 1960's. Many chapels closed down and became shops, factories or even homes.

The Providence Place Congregational Chapel has become home to what is reputed to be the largest Indian restaurant in the world; The Aakash. The Upper Independent Chapel in Heckmondwike has been transformed into luxury apartments.

In 1953, a Roman Catholic Church was built in Cleckheaton, St Paul's Church, but this was the exception to the rule.

Anglican worship continued at Birstall, Hartshead and Whitechapel and all the 'newer' churches built in the 19th Century. Many chapels have also survived from the great wave of chapel building of the 19th Century, and for those Christians still practising their religion into the 21st Century, there continues to be the Sunday services, the weekly social activities and the baptisms, weddings and funeral services which have been the way of life of local communities for hundreds of years. Now there are the same number of churches and chapels within the Spen Valley.

There is also a trend for incorporating areas within churches and chapels which can be used as kitchens, cafes and meeting rooms. Places of worship are the centres of the community once again.

In Scholes village, the numbers attending the Quaker Meeting House decreased until by the end of 1960, the group of Friends had become so small that the meeting house was closed and the little group joined the Brighouse Meeting. In 1966, it was re-opened for meetings and exhibitions to show visitors what kind of work the Quakers do.

It is now, once again a place of worship. Three hundred years after the Society of Friends was established in the Spen Valley, the Quaker religion remains. As does the Moravian Church.

Other Religions

As well as offering Homes Fit For Heroes to British participants in the Second World War, Britain also offered a homeland for the Heroes of the Empire who had fought in the British army in many parts of the world.

Thousands of Muslim soldiers were killed or wounded while fighting for British rights and liberties. An exhibition at the Times Past museum at the Ponderosa Rare Breeds Centre in Heckmondwike, shows the massive contribution made by former black Afro-Caribbean and South-East Asian soldiers of the British Empire, fighting alongside the allies in both world wars.

In the late 1950's, many families from S.E. Asia, particularly Pakistan, settled in parts of the West Riding of Yorkshire and some of these settled in Heckmondwike. Life was not easy for them. They didn't speak English very well and they had to adapt to a very different way of life and to the cold weather! Many were well educated but had to find work in poorly paid manual jobs. Many of the local men returning from the war were determined not to go back to work in the mills and the immigrants filled their places. They also took on the work of running convenience stores which opened for long hours to serve the needs of local communities.

At first Muslims gathered in their homes for prayer and worship. The prayer mat was their temporary mosque. Later, mosques were built, like the Jamia Mosque on Jeremy Lane, Heckmondwike. We now have a multi-cultural population and therefore a multi-faith population. Just as in the past when we had a multitude of Nonconformist faiths; Independents, Congregationalists, Quakers, Moravians and others, we now have a far larger variety of beliefs. Kirklees Faiths Forum is an organisation which helps to unite faith communities so that we can learn from each other.

CHANGES IN SHOPPING HABITS

Shopping became a leisure activity for the first time at the turn of the 20th Century. Family businesses became larger with far more staff, men and women. Bakers shops expanded and Heckmondwike and Cleckheaton boasted tea-rooms. Grocers stores showed off lavish displays and more and more goods were now packaged.

During the First World War, women had to run the shops when the men were conscripted into the services. They proved themselves very capable and this was one more way in which women were empowered by the war.

During the Second World War they were left alone again to staff the shops and this time they had the additional task of sorting out the ration books.

Until the 1960's, the Co-op and the family businesses, including corner shops, were the only sort of shops around. The Co-op was still the largest in the Spen Valley.

Branches like the one in Heckmondwike which faced the park, had lots of departments There was a chemist department, and optical, confectionery and grocers departments. There would also be haberdashery, and of course the butchers. In addition there would be shoes, drapers, tailoring, jewellery, furnishing and very importantly the funeral directors!

Hillards

John Wesley Hillard was an example of a local family shopkeeper. He opened his first shop, a corner shop, in 1885 (with a £50 loan) in a building called Lion Chambers on the new high street, Northgate in Cleckheaton.

Within a few years he opened four more shops in the Spen Valley area and then expanded his chain until by the early 20th Century there were well over twenty shops all trading under the name Lion Stores. In 1922, he bought a rival chain of thirteen shops trading as Jubb's Grocers.

In the Great Depression years of the 1930's, he opened a number of small shops selling only a limited range of basic goods. These traded as Park Stores because the first was situated opposite the park in Heckmondwike. By the time of his death in 1935, there were over sixty shops trading as Lion's Stores.

From the start, he was an innovator.

He provided tea and biscuits and return tram fares home to his early customers. He also moved with the times and when people had little money to spend, he geared his shops to their basic needs.

In his own way, John Wesley Hillard was as entrepreneurial as the leaders of industry and like many of them he had a philanthropic attitude to his workforce.

His family continued to innovate.

In the 1950's mobile shops were introduced. Then in 1952, the first self-service store opened in Brighouse; only the second of its kind in the whole of Yorkshire. Within ten years all the shops had been converted to self-service and the Hillard family built a warehouse and headquarters in Spen Lane to keep up with the new requirement for buying on a large scale.

In 1970 they began trading as Hillards and under the management of JW's grandsons, David and Peter Hartley, expanded into the Midlands, Derbyshire, Lancashire and Lincolnshire.

In 1972 the annual sales were more than £300 million and some of their supermarkets were the largest and most modern in the country with in-store bakers, cafes and petrol stations. Over 7,500 people worked in the Company and more than 4,000 were shareholders.

Then in May 1987, an unwelcome and fiercely contested bid by Tesco ended a hundred years of family service to the Spen Valley and beyond.

Supermarkets

While the Sixties saw the start of supermarkets, the Eighties was the decade of their consolidation into the few very large names we are familiar with today.

By this time most people owned freezers and did their shopping weekly, not daily. They also expected to buy lots of their non- food items in these shops. In addition most people had cars and so could easily carry a week's supply of food home. In other words, it was convenient.

So supermarkets take far more of the total expenditure now than in earlier decades. The Spen Valley has two such large organisations. One is Morrisons in Heckmondwike (which has a fairly local man as its founder, Ken Morrison from Bradford). The other is Tesco in Cleckheaton which has its links with our very own JW Hillard!

The trend for bigger and bigger supermarkets and out of town shopping outlets, as well as internet shopping, has had inevitable effects on the once thriving towns of Heckmondwike and Cleckheaton making it difficult for smaller specialist shops to survive. This is a cause for concern because the streets of towns are the heart of the communities where people can meet up. It's also a fact that most people like to interact with shopkeepers. They also like the range of goods in the specialist shops and the advice and service they can get from local shopkeepers.

CHANGES IN INDUSTRY

The main change was that the traditional industries declined throughout the 20th Century. The 1930's Depression saw the closure of many mills. Some villages, like Birkenshaw, saw the collapse of their two biggest mills. Other areas survived by diversifying and indeed many new industries emerged. This was a very positive change. The development for the first time in the history of the Spen Valley, of completely new industries meant that there was still employment for local people.

BBA (British Belting and Asbestos)

The biggest newcomer on the industrial scene arrived at the very start of the century. In 1901, John Fenton and Walter Corbett bought Savile Mills in Cleckheaton and re-named it Scandinavia Mills.

It became the Spen Valley's largest employer. Fenton had invented a solid twill woven belt for driving machinery back in 1879 and had gone into partnership with Walter Corbet to sell it. The business thrived because Corbett, the salesman of the partnership, had extended sales all around the world. The solid woven belting was in great demand, being used for power transmission and mechanical conveying in industries and in mining.

Hence the need to move to the large premises in Cleckheaton.

From 1908 the company became involved in the automotive trade and Henry Ford was one of the first to put in orders for belting for the gearbox of his Model T. This was followed by orders from Morris, Austin and Vauxhall in the UK and Renault and Bugatti in France.

When the First World War broke out, Government orders took priority and production was switched to khaki and brace webbing for the British army. In addition, belting was provided for a French rifle manufacturer.

During the inter-war years, the company's automotive and friction products business developed under the brand name Mintex.

When the Second World War started in 1939, the British military's need for woven materials resulted in another period of increased activity. The workforce increased from 403 to 1,400. Mintex products were key components in most British warplanes (over 90% of the total supplies of brake linings for Spitfires, Hurricanes, Typhoons and Wellingtons). Mintex materials were also fitted to many of the tanks, whose steering depended on their brakes. Army webbing, parachute harnesses and fire hoses were all woven on the company's looms.

After the war, the company's automotive and friction products business developed further. It played a key role in the development of disc brake pads and in fact was the world's largest supplier. By the 1960's the company owned subsidiaries in many parts of the world. By the 1970's they had launched a company making material for the construction industry.

When the BBA celebrated its centenary in 1979, the site had grown to about 30 acres, including the factory buildings as well as the research and development department.

In the 1980's, the BBA Group made its move into the aviation business, making landing gear and hydraulic systems. Throughout the 1990's it continued to develop this side of the business and this was the time that they re-structured what was now a world wide industrial conglomerate and the Cleckheaton site was closed.

For nearly a hundred years, the BBA had played a major role in the Spen Valley. The company has had four Royal visitors during its history. In 1932, the Duke of York (the future King George VI), in 1943 the Princess Royal and in 1949, Princess Elizabeth (Queen Elizabeth) toured the works. In December 1975, Prince Charles was able to see, on his visit, the biggest belting loom in the world which had twelve 40 inch beams, each of which held more than a ton of yarn: a total of over 100,000 miles!

Motorbikes

Joah Carver Phelon, whose factory in Cleckheaton, produced metal dies for the wire drawing industry, designed and built a motor car in 1896. Unfortunately it crashed on its test run!

Phelon was a keen cyclist and he decided to attach a motor to a bicycle. He took the strongest cycle frame he could find and began to build his motorbike. It was completed in 1901. In 1904 he formed Phelon and Moore, in partnership with Richard Moore with £250 capital.

In 1910, they built Horncastle Mills in Cleckheaton. When the First World War broke out they started making motorcycles for the Royal Flying Corps and they continued this after 1918 when the RFC became the RAF. In fact they were the exclusive suppliers.

In the early 1920's, they began building their famous Panther model which had some successes in the Isle-of-Man TT races. In the 1930's, they produced their famous Red Panther which sold for twenty nine pounds, seventeen shillings and sixpence; a price within the range of the working class man.

During the Second World War, they produced aviation components, resuming the motorcycle production in 1946 with a single-cylinder engine and top speed of 80 mph. This made them the ideal engines to be attached to the family sidecars, a popular and cheap form of transport for the working class family. Sadly, they had to cease production in 1967 because of competition from Japanese manufacturers.

Panther motorcycles, Savoy Square, Cleckheaton

Motor Cars

Cleckheaton became the centre for another motor industry when Abel Blackburn started production of his four wheel, 10hp Norfolk car.

It had solid tyres, a 2 cylinder engine and could reach the amazing speeds of 40 mph! The rate of travel was adjusted by a three speed gear box. The chassis was produced in Cleckheaton and then fitted with the coachwork in Barnsley.

There were no huge profits for Abe in those early days of car production so when a big order for textile machinery came in from South America, he had to choose between financial loss or security.

But there is a story told by his grand-children of his meeting with Henry Royce of the Rolls-Royce partnership to discuss possible co-operation.

Abe Blackburn only produced 14 Norfolk cars at his factory at Tofts Mill in Serpentine Road. Production ended in 1905, but it was quite an achievement for a small town like Cleckheaton. Blackburn and Co Ltd was a textile machinery manufacturers but at the time Abe thought that making cars was much simpler than the complicated carding machines they were producing!

The only surviving Norfolk was restored in 1933 and in 2004 it made its 50th appearance in the London to Brighton vintage rally. It has also made another appearance; as one of the feature film posters in Savoy square, Cleckheaton. In 2008, Abel Blackburn's grand-daughter and her husband travelled from the South of England to see it.

Confectionery

The Lion Confectionery Company was founded in 1903 by Frank and Albert Hardill who made pastilles, and gums like midget gems. Their most famous sweet was named Poor Ben, it's said after the man who first sampled it!

Their factory is still at South Parade on Westgate in Cleckheaton. All the weighing and wrapping of sweets was done by hand (mainly by women) right up to 1991 when a roll-wrap machine took over.

Some of the delights of the factory were liquorice sticks, lemon squash gums, Guy Fawkes bonfire toffee and old fashioned humbugs. Thousands of tonnes of gum-based sweets are still produced here every year.

The factory still uses a steam boiler installed back in 1926 which goes by the affectionate name of Helen. In 1986, the Hardill Family sold the business to Cadbury's. The factory changed hands again in 2008 when it was bought by the Blackpool based Tangerine Confectionery. The best line is still Lion's midget gems which are now exported all the way to Australia.

Another confectionery firm was set up in Oxford Road Gomersal, by Walter Smith who founded Toffee Smith's. He began his business by selling penny toffee bars to churches as fundraisers. This firm closed in the 1990's.

THE TRADITIONAL FACTORIES

The Goliath Boot and Shoe Company

This Company, founded by the Co-operative Wholesale Society in 1880, continued to flourish in the factory on Brunswick Street, Heckmondwike. It was still manufacturing hard wearing work boots but it was now supplying specialist footwear for British Aerospace, Rolls Royce and the Coal Board among others. Around 400 workers produced between 6,000 and 8,000 pairs of boots every week. One of the most famous products was the lightweight football boots made for Sir Stanley Matthews who made several visits to the factory.

Very often members of the same family worked at Goliath. A retired worker talked about how he was one of eleven children and he and four of his brothers as well as his father worked for the company.

They all lived in the terraced houses nearby. He described the different departments. The basement was where the tanning took place. The ground floor was where the soles were cut on massive presses. On the top floor the patterns were cut and machined, mainly by women. Then the partly made up shoes and boots were taken down to the first floor where they were made up on Lasts. His wife worked at Firth's Carpets and she had been brought up on the Firthcliffe Estate.

In 2003, the CWS sold Goliath Footwear and the factory closed down. The products of this famous factory are now made abroad. However a distribution warehouse exists on the former BBA site in Cleckheaton.

The Textile Mills

Some mills remained. For example, Burnley's in Gomersal which had started back in 1753, remained one of the biggest in the Spen Valley. Then in 1996, it too closed down and the business was transferred to Ireland.

But carpets are still made in Heckmondwike. FB Ltd operates from Wellington Mills and is now a leading specialist manufacturer of heavy contract fibre-bonded carpets. Westex Carpets produce high quality carpets at Moorend, Cleckheaton and sells its carpets all over the world. It is one of the biggest employers in Cleckheaton. Another large carpet firm is Fibre Bonded Carpets and Tiles in Liversedge.

There are still several yarn suppliers like Millbridge Spinning Co. Ltd in Liversedge which is a Carpet Yarn manufacturer, importing wool from all over the world and carding and spinning it before sending it to be dyed. Their finest (white) wool comes from New Zealand.

This factory occupies what used to be Cooke's Mill 'A.' At the intersection of the three roads was Mill 'B,' and to it's right was Mill 'C.'

Mill 'A' was always involved in the spinning process but Mills 'B' and 'C' were involved in the weaving of carpets when Cooke's were in business.

Typically there are workmen's cottages across the road from the Mill. And also of interest is that the latest part of Mill 'A' occupies the site of the old corn mill from the 18th Century which took the place of the medieval corn mill at the point where the Ashton-Clough Beck flows into the Spen River.

Millbridge Spinning Co. Ltd. Liversedge

Lingcroft Associates Ltd in Cleckheaton is another survivor of the textile industry. This is one of Europe's leading suppliers of fabrics for uniforms. And more technical products are supplied at Fybagrate in Liversedge. This manufactures non-woven needle felts using a wide variety of fibres.

Biscor Ltd in Oakenshaw is one of the world's largest and most innovative producers of high performance coated fabrics, for example Teflon coated and silicone rubber-coated fabric used in a wide variety of industries.

Engineering Works

Some of these remained into the 20th Century. The Pyenot Hall Works in Cleckheaton joined British Ropes Ltd in 1924 and then in 1974 they re-organised and formed Bridon Ltd which manufactured the strands for pre-stressing concrete, in particular for the pre-stressing of oil production platforms in the North Sea.

This firm closed down but plenty more engineering works have survived into the 21st Century and adapted to meet changing demands, such as 600 Lathes in Heckmondwike. This firm was formed in London in 1932 where its head office address was 600, Commercial Road. It became the UK's leading lathe manufacturer after buying Colchester Lathes in 1954 and TS Harrison in Heckmondwike in 1971. It specialises in manufacturing state of the art machine tools and products. It also makes precision engineered components, laser marking systems and mechanical handling and waste management equipment. It sells its products all over the world and in 2011 acquired another plant in Poland.

Arthur Heaton and Company, also in Heckmondwike, is still a leading manufacturer of reels and drums for the wire and cable industry.

Flexitallic Ltd is a large manufacturer of industrial sealants in Cleckheaton. It celebrated its centenary in 2012. It produces different types of metallic gaskets, ring-type joints and such like. Kautex Textron (UK) Ltd manufactures vehicle components in Liversedge.

Garnett Wire Ltd, founded in 1851 in Scholes is now the only manufacturer of metallic card clothing in the UK and still supplies the textile manufacturers of the world. And Foxton Dies Ltd in Westgate, Cleckheaton makes wire drawing dies for many operations in industry, for example, re-inforced concrete, jewellery, steel cord for tyres etc.

The engineering industry, just like the textile industry, still exists in the Spen Valley.

The End of Coalmining

Coalmining, however has disappeared completely from the Valley. By 1970 only Gomersal Colliery remained. This was a 20th Century pit, the first shaft being sunk in 1911. Conditions were always bad and up to 1951 all coal was worked with picks and shovels. The 1960's was a very profitable decade and the managers had to introduce a little train for the miners to get to work as the coal face had moved so far away from the mine head, plus a conveyor belt for the coal. But by 1973 the coalmine had to be closed down for fear of flooding.

The spoil heaps were landscaped into Oakwell Hall Country Park. The only reminder of a once thriving coal mine is the Miners' Memorial. This is a sculpture on the spot where the coolie car engine house to the drift mine once stood. Here, the miners boarded the train to take them to the coal face. It was erected by the Spen Valley Civic Society as a permanent memory of the industry. Now it's where families leave their cars and wander off to enjoy the amenities of the park.

Miners' Memorial. Oakwell Hall Country Park

INDUSTRY TODAY

One thing that has changed is that is that young people no longer start as apprentices and stay in the same job for life, often with other members of their family. Now many people have to change jobs and re-train several times in their working lives just to keep abreast of changing circumstances.

Another change has been that jobs in the service industries have multiplied. Also people travel longer distances to their place of work. This puts a great strain on the road networks and necessitates more and more initiatives to deal with the problems of transport.

There are still managers of businesses however who continue in the manner of those early entrepreneurs of the Spen Valley; men who from the 19th Century onwards have left their legacy in so many ways. New industries are still replacing the old. The difference is that they no longer employ the huge numbers that were needed in the past. An example of a new industry in the Spen Valley is the firm of Ferno in Cleckheaton. This is the world's leading manufacturer of medical equipment to the emergency services and funeral sector. This company exports to over ninety five countries worldwide.

The tradition of diversity and flexibility has helped reduce the severity of economic recessions which can cripple towns dependent on only one industry. Many firms have adapted to meet the new challenges in the 21st Century just as industries in the past forged ahead, led by enterprising men.

BIRKBY'S PLASTICS LTD, LIVERSEDGE

This is a company which illustrates the point until very recently. Arnold and Freddie Birkby established their firm in 1867. They were pioneers of industry. Their success shows how entrepreneurs can adapt to changing circumstances.

They began as textile machinery manufacturers but at the beginning of the 20th Century, they took notice of the fact that trams were the boom industry and so they began producing overhead line materials and electrical insulation.

During the First World War, the brothers worked with the Belgian inventor of Bakelite, Leo Baekland, and became the first British firm to manufacture Bakelite articles. This evolved into the manufacture of plastics.

The company was well placed to latch on to the next boom industry, the automotive industry. They started to make dashboards, fuse assembly boxes, light reflectors, clutch discs and brake linings. Their biggest customer was London Passenger Transport.

In 1926, the brothers started producing telephone handsets for the GPO and then the parts for the next new industry, the wireless; plastic casings, knobs, valve bases, coil bobbins and loudspeakers. In the 1950's the company started making thermoplastics (Acrylic).

The last of the Birkby family retired in 1958 but the name was kept. And the business kept on going.

In the 1960's it was taken over by the Plessey Company and expanded into the defence, avionics and electronics industry. It has had several owners since but with each company the firm has prospered.

Until 2012 it designed, manufactured and assembled components for the car industry. For more than twenty years it has supplied interior parts for Jaguar, Nissan and other car manufacturers and has been a flourishing firm, receiving prestigious awards for quality and delivery performance.

Always a pioneer in its field, always fortunate in having a loyal, skilled workforce often made up of members of the same family.

Constant evolution and innovation ensured its success.

That is until the deepest recession in recent times brought to an end this historic firm with such an illustrious past.

This is only one of the many stories over the centuries of entrepreneurs in the Spen Valley, who could spot trends and develop them into opportunities.

And finally, a company which was not home-grown...

OWENS-CORNING VEIL LTD, LIVERSEDGE

This company is a market leader in glass fibre technology, making fibres out of glass and not textiles.

It was founded in 1938 in the USA and is now a world wide company. It has factories in North America, Europe and Asia and two factories in the UK; one in Lancaster and one here in Liversedge.

These factories make glass fibre materials which can be found in over 40,000 products ranging from telecommunications, cables, boats, aircraft, automobiles, computers, building construction and many others.

The Lancaster factory produces automotive products and the Liversedge factory concentrates on non-woven technology. It celebrated its 25th Anniversary in 2012.

Two interesting facts emerge here.

Firstly, this factory is at the top of Hare Park Lane where it joins Halifax Road, on the site of factories and workshops from long ago. This is where Rayner's Mill stood, one of the large textile mills of the 19th Century.

By the end of that century the factory owner had built a row of terrace house for his workers, still called Rayners Avenue, and a row of manager's villas, also on Hare Park Lane.

This is also the site of Jackson's cropping shop from where the Luddites recruited many of the men who took that fateful journey on the night of 11th April 1812. And even further back, it was the site of the workshop owned by the original Rayner family who came to England with the Flemish weavers in the 14th Century.

The second interesting fact to note is how industry today is a worldwide affair. Spen Valley industries grew out of the environment and were often inter-dependent. Now the world is a much smaller place and businesses can reach into every corner.

This world leading producer has its home in Liversedge. And on an industrial site which goes back into history.

CHAPTER 15: LOOKING BACK

The historic townships of Liversedge, Cleckheaton, Heckmondwike and Gomersal are unlike most.

There is not a single unit growing out of one town centre. Spenborough was formed by the growing together of small towns, villages and hamlets, each with its own traditions, identities and a sense of local independence.

The inhabitants of these townships have always been stubbornly independent-minded. We have seen this from the earliest resistance to the Norman Overlords after 1066 all the way through to the strong support for Parliament against a tyrannical King in the civil wars of the 17th Century. This spirit was seen too in the embracing of Nonconformism in the 17th and 18th Centuries and in the actions of the machine breakers, the Plug Drawers and the Chartists in the 19th Century. It continued with involvement in left wing politics in the 20th Century; first with the Liberals and then the Socialists.

We have had our fair share of philanthropists among the dwellers of the valley.

The Essolfs gave generously to the crusading knights. The Quakers and Moravians followed their calling and helped communities like Liversedge, Scholes, Little Gomersal and Wyke to develop.

The millowners played their part in the 19th Century. Many of them were Nonconformists and Anglicans who built the chapels and churches which provided communities with education and social amenities. Their religion imbued them with a strong sense of moral values.

There were many benefactors too, like the Mowat Family, in the 20th Century who donated a Library to the people of Spenborough in 1930 and who gifted their family home as a Cheshire Home to provide residential care for disabled people from across Kirklees in 1960.

There has been plenty of scientific and engineering talent over the years. Joseph Priestley, the eminent 18th Century scientist became a world renowned figure.

There have been all the creative minds involved in the products of industry and transport in the last two centuries. Many local entrepreneurs invented machinery to help maximise the products of the mills and the means of motorised transport.

John Fozard continued this trend into the 20th Century. He was an old boy of Heckmondwike Grammar School and between 1963 and 1978, he became design chief for the Harrier Jump Jet.

We have had our share of famous sportsmen and women too. Jeff Butterfield, who was born in Heckmondwike, played rugby for England in the 1950's, winning 28 consecutive caps for his country. John Bentley, from Cleckheaton, also played rugby for England in the 1990's.

Lisa Brambani, from Hartshead, was a famous Olympic cyclist in the 1980's and 1990's, and Tim Bresnan from Gomersal and Andrew Gale from Hartshead are renowned cricketers.

There has also been plenty of artistic talent. Edward Wadsworth son of the millowner of Broomfield Mill, was one of England's greatest 20th Century artists and he was born in Cleckheaton.

Ken Macintosh, the famous band leader, was born near the Town Hall in Liversedge, and Arthur Wood of Heckmondwike, composed the theme tune for 'The Archers.'

And last but by no means least Roger Hargreaves, creator of the *Mr Men* was born in Hightown. His books have delighted children from the 1970's onwards. He was brought up in a semi-detached house on Halifax Road, Hightown. In 1971 he produced his first book called 'Mr. Tickle' after his youngest son Adam asked what a tickle looked like. After his death in 1988, his son Adam continued to write more books in the series. These books have become world famous.

All the incomers have made the Spen Valley what it is today; from the Angles, Saxons, Vikings and Normans in the early middle ages; the Flemings from the 14th Century; refugees from war-torn Europe in the 20th Century and the Asian and East European immigrants who came here after the Second World War.

History is always in the making. It's the creation of the people themselves.

As an incomer myself, I hope that this book reflects some of my pride in being associated with such a place and that it gives others some of the pleasure that I have gained from understanding why the Spen Valley has developed the way it has.

Books and Sources:

General:

- Spen Valley Past and Present: Frank Peel
- Spen Valley: A Landscape of Hamlets: Scargill and Lee
- History of the Spen Valley: 1780's to 1980: Douglas Hird
- The Place Names of the West Riding of Yorkshire: AH Smith
- Life and Tradition in West Yorkshire: M Hartley and J Ingelby
- The Making of the English Working Class: EP Thompson
- The Making of the English Landscape: WG Hoskins

Churches:

- A History of Hartshead: Mabel Ferrett
- Hartshead and District in Times Past: Margaret Wood
- The Church on the Hill: A Century of Restoration: 1981 Leaflet
- A Thousand Years of Worship: St Peter's Church Birstall: KR O'Shea

Cleckheaton:

- Cleckheaton in Times Past: Margaret Wood
- Cleckheaton Chapels: E Wood (Bradford Family History Society)
- Oakenshaw: A Paper by Maureen Orme (Cleckheaton Archives)
- From Scales to Scholes: David Wilding

Liversedge:

- Liversedge Town Books: Cleckheaton Library (1678, 1811, 1826)
- Hanson Papers: Copies and translations of the medieval manuscripts and deeds relating to Liversedge in the Bodlean Library made by John Hanson, Solicitor of Rastrick (Cleckheaton Library)
- Dendrochronological Analysis of Oak Timbers from Haigh House Liversedge: Dr Andy Muir, May 2012

Gomersal:

- The Birch Grove: Philip Mallpress
- A Window on the Past: Gillian and Neil Cookson
- A Brief History of Spen Hall: P Scraton
- Oakwell Hall: Geoffrey Wedge
- Life Dahn't Pit: The Spen Valley Civic Society

Nonconformism:

- Nonconformism in the Spen Valley: Frank Peel
- 150th Anniversary Souvenier of St John's Methodist Church Hightown (Cleckheaton Reference Library)
- A History of Quakerism in Liversedge and Scholes: David Blamires

The Brontes:

- The Brontes: Mabel Ferrett
- The Taylors of Red House: Mabel Ferrett
- The Life of Charlotte Bronte: Elizabeth Gaskell
- Shirley: Charlotte Bronte

The Luddites:

- Liberty or Death: Alan Brooke and Lesley Kipling
- The Risings of the Luddites: Frank Peel
- The Luddites: Douglas Liversedge
- The Luddites: James Berry
- Land of Lost Content: Robert Reid
- Lord Byron's Maiden Speech, February 27th 1812 (Hansard)
- Documents relating to the attack on Rawfolds Mill (Leeds Mercury, April 18th 1812)
- The visiting of the families of Luddite sufferers in the area of Huddersfield: Joseph Wood, a Yorkshire Quaker (Joseph Wood Manuscript Diary)

Industry

- 150th Anniversary of Flush Mills Heckmondwike, TF Firth and Sons (Cleckheaton Reference Library)
- Primary evidence concerning the history of the Old Silk Mill Gomersal (provided by Simon Green, with permission from the Stevenson family)
- Primary evidence concerning Hare Park Mills (provided by the present owner, Mr. Ralph G. Wilson)

Two World Wars:

- One Valley's War: Andrew Bannister
- Words On War: Helga Hughes
- Archives of the Spenborough Guardian 1939-1945
- Local Archives in Cleckheaton Library
- West Yorkshire Archives, Huddersfield Library

The Spen in Springtime

And the stories and information handed to me from the many interesting people I have met as I have done my fieldwork especially the owners of some of the fascinating houses of the Valley; Mr. and Mrs. Franklyn of Liversedge Hall and Mr. and Mrs. Wilkinson of Haigh House and the staff at Hollybank School (Roe Head). Also Craig Oldroyd of Middle Hall, Mrs. Wilkinson of Headlands Hall and the owners of Peel Hall, Lowfold Hall, Lower Blacup Farm and Upper House Farm and many others including staff of Millbridge Spinning Co; Janet, Joanne and Shane and retired workers of former factories, for example the Co-op Boot and Shoe Company and for Kalon Ltd for their kind permission to allow me to photograph the Rydings House.

Particular thanks go to:

Staff at the West Yorkshire Archive Service in Huddersfield for their help with maps; tithe maps, enclosure maps, Township maps, surveys and valuation books.

Staff at Red House Museum and Oakwell Hall

Jim Summerscales for drawing the maps needed for this book. (Jim's great grandfather x 3 was James Lister, landlord of The Shears Inn in 1812).

Dr. John Hargreaves for his series of lectures on The Luddites in the Local Landscape, Literature and History Workers: Educational Association (meeting at Red House)

Donald Haigh (MA FSA) Retired Master for Archaeology, Bradford Grammar School, for his input on the Roman Roads of the Spen Valley.

Yvonne Luke from English Heritage for a site visit and information on the Walton Cross

The Spen Valley Civic Society for their inspirational books, pamphlets and projects which do so much to keep the spirit of history alive in the Valley.

And finally, many thanks go to my family, particularly my husband David, who has accompanied me on my many travels while researching the book, my son Richard who has prepared the book for printing, my daughter Caroline who has arranged the printing and my nephew John for his bricks on the wall montage.

And... Nina, who is now the only dog expert on The Spen Valley Story!